CHESHIRE V.C.

Cheshire V.C.

Russell Braddon

WHITE LION PUBLISHERS LIMITED
London, New York, Sydney and Toronto

Copyright © Russell Braddon, 1954

First published by Evans Brothers Ltd., 1954

White Lion Edition, 1975

Made and printed in
Great Britain
for White Lion Publishers Limited,
138 Park Lane, London W1Y 3DD
by
R. Kingshott & Co. Ltd.,
Deadbrook Lane, Aldershot, Hampshire.

To

JUDY AND JIM

who discussed all I've written here a
thousand times, read it twice and always
brought me company at the right times.

CONTENTS

LIST OF ILLUSTRATIONS
Between pages 98 and 99

The photographs are reproduced by permission of the Air Ministry, Associated Press, Central Press, Mrs. G. C. Cheshire, Imperial War Museum, Kemsley Newspapers, London News Agency, Mirropic, *News Chronicle*, P. A. Reuter, *Picture Post* and Charles White.

PROLOGUE

No two personal experiences of war could have been more different than those of Group Captain Leonard Cheshire, V.C., and myself. The V.C. itself quickly establishes that!

I was a prisoner-of-war of the Japanese. As such my war began with humiliation, continued with disease and degradation and ended abruptly with a release to the joyous recapture of freedom and health.

Leonard Cheshire, on the other hand, began his war with exultation, continued it with distinction and concluded it with the shadow of an atomic cloud lying heavily on his mind and the fate of savage ill-health in store.

Yet these war-time experiences we share. The lesson that one's fellow men and women are infinitely more valuable than any other material possession: the knowledge that their courage and spiritual grandeur can rise above any physical stress: and the impact upon our lives of the explosion, in warfare, of the atomic bomb.

In this last respect, however, we reacted for different reasons. We, the prisoners of the Japanese, because only the abrupt and utterly unexpected termination of hostilities brought about by its use saved us from the extermination our captors had so callously planned for us. Cheshire, the war-time hero of a hundred operational flights against the European enemy, because he recognized the atomic bomb instantly for what it was—the ultimate threat of man's own godless inventiveness against man. He recognized this so swiftly and surely because he has rare qualities both of perception and intelligence, and because he was there.

This much I knew I shared with Leonard Cheshire. When I met him for the first time I learnt that we shared an experience of something else, mine in the past and his at this very moment, and that is a close personal acquaintance with physical suffering. And because he has learnt the lesson that all we prisoners of the Japanese had to learn if we were to survive—that suffering doesn't matter ("it doesn't matter," we declared to ourselves, "none of this matters")—because he, too, has learnt this lesson, I felt an affinity to the man, which our achievements and records would certainly never warrant.

At once I decided that the story I wanted to write was not the story, raid by raid, statistical fact upon statistical fact, of Group Captain Cheshire, V.C., but rather the story of Leonard Cheshire the man.

I wanted to paint him as he is. Not a Royal Academy portrait, elegant in its formality and empty of experience and character, but an honest drawing, harsh lines, faults and all, which would let other people see him as clearly as he has allowed me to do—and he is a man of devastating honesty about himself.

Here then is no conventional biography. I went cynically to him, as an agnostic reporter prepared to meet (for many had briefed me about him) a religious fanatic who was "round the bend."

I went curiously to him, to see this man who was so impressively decorated. I expected someone at least nine feet tall and unspeakably aloof.

I went eagerly, hoping for the war story of all time.

Instead I found the sanest and most contented man, tuberculosis notwithstanding, I have ever known. I found a slightly built man of ordinary appearance and quite extraordinary charm: I *got* my story: and it was a story not of war but of Peace. That is the message which I have tried to pass on in this book. And if I have succeeded, don't praise me, praise Cheshire, for practically every word in it is his.

RUSSELL BRADDON

Chapter One

THE TURNING POINT

H E WAS AN English Group Captain, yet he flew in the nose of an American B.29, flew at 39,000 feet, in brilliant sunshine, over Japan: flew àt four hundred miles an hour to observe the dropping of one bomb on one city. The greatest war mankind has ever known, the first global war, had only six days left to run: and Nagasaki, a proud city, had less than two minutes left to live. It was August 9th, 1945, and Leonard Cheshire was about to witness the explosion of the war's second atomic bomb.

Sitting in the bomb-aimer's seat, he presented a curiously contradictory picture. He looked very young, with his brown hair parted in the middle and brushed flat and backwards. His eyes were clear and sparkled but they held a grim wariness in their depths, and the smile that came so easily to his lips was often not reflected in those eyes. He was slim, which added to his youthfulness: he was serious, in a shy kind of way, and so did that.

But his slimness was partly a taut, burnt-out exhaustion, and his seriousness was partly a profound and too-premature wisdom, and these things gave him an aged authority which somehow lay oddly on the brow of one who still, at twenty-seven, looked a boy. Expertly he surveyed the scene beyond and below the perspex blister in which he sat. His expression was a mixture of enthusiastic excitement and experience which was immune to all surprise.

Below them Japan seemed unperturbed. There was no hostile fire, no sign of ground activity, no enemy aircraft to molest them. Perhaps they had not been seen. Or perhaps, although seen, the knowledge that only two Super-Fortresses flew over their ancient island nation had decided the Japanese that no harm could come from them.

Indeed, one would not expect harm from the sight presented by a B.29 at 39,000 feet. They look silvery, translucent and ethereal at that height. But never had their appearance been more deluding than on this day: never had the groundling's impression of a lulling rhythmic roar, so characteristic of the B.29's four Boeing engines, been more treacherously deceptive. For one of the planes came to murder a complete city: the second came to watch. In this second plane flew Leonard Cheshire.

Everything about the flight was strange to him, doubly strange because, to a man like himself (the most decorated bomber pilot in the Royal Air Force, flyer of one hundred missions against enemy Europe), there should be no surprises left in the realm of air warfare; and yet constantly he was surprised.

He sat in shirt sleeves and was warm, though they flew at great height. This was strange to a pilot whose Lancasters and Halifaxes had registered interior temperatures of 16° below zero at altitudes less than a third of that which, so steadily and effortlessly, they maintained now. The Super-Fortress was pressurized and heated—unheard-of luxury to British pilots, in whose planes comfort had been ruthlessly sacrificed to economy and production output and who expected not warmth but rain drips, ice and arctic draughts.

He wore no oxygen mask and plugged in no intercom: yet he breathed naturally and conversed freely with the American crew, who roamed the inside of their plane with easy informality. And this, too, was strange.

But strangest of all was the fact that he flew at 39,000 feet, he who hated heights, although he was acknowledged to be Britain's greatest bomber pilot, her finest air leader, and had three D.S.O.s, a D.F.C. and the Victoria Cross to prove it.

Ironically he reflected how, when he had first flown a bomber to Italy, he had remarked to himself that 15,000 feet was a horrifying altitude and much higher than any of his late friends like Jimmy and Lofty and Lousy, like Frammy and Willy, Revs and Taffy, had ever flown.

They were all dead, of course, all of his first war-time colleagues: but they had never flown at 15,000 feet over the Alps, still less at 39,000 feet over Japan. They would be surprised, could they see their "Chesh" now; Chesh, of all people, seven miles up in the air.

They were all dead, though. The earth, even Japanese earth, looked so remote and detached, way down there beyond him, that he grew unusually nostalgic for the past and the steadfast, cheery aircrew members who had once been his friends.

Not many more than Munro and Dave Shannon and Mick Martin now survived—that was very few out of the scores he had known so long and so well. Terribly few when he remembered how indestructible some of them had seemed. Jimmy for instance. Jimmy had been killed in 1941. Jimmy who flew so superbly. But then it wasn't skill that saved you in the war, at least, not skill alone. It was luck. That was how he had got through. He was lucky. Everyone knew it. "Cheshire is lucky," they said, aircrew and ground crew alike. So he survived one hundred missions which, statistically speaking, should have seen him dead four times, and now he flew over Japan on his hundred and first.

He looked at the soil below him without compassion. It was enemy soil: the people on it were the enemy. The more of their country that was devastated, and the more of their numbers destroyed, the sooner the war would end. And the sooner it ended the greater would be the saving in the Allied lives required to win it.

He knew that they were going to drop a very unusual bomb because he had worked on the project in the Mariana Islands for months beforehand. He had even become infected by the obsessive enthusiasm of the American crews who were to go on this mission. So obsessed had they been that they had lived in terror for days lest the Japanese should surrender *before* they could drop their bomb on Nagasaki.

There had even been a frivolous suggestion (humorous in its expression—but mortally serious in its sentiment) that, should this dire misfortune of a premature end to hostilities befall them, they should take off without permission and bomb Nagasaki nevertheless.

He had been told about the bomb too. How it would explode, where it would explode, what would happen when it did explode. The Americans had been vastly informative, in their customary generous fashion. And an English scientist called Dr. William Penney, who flew with him now as the only other non-American observer, had gone to great pains to explain what was meant by an atomic explosion with its chain reaction and its nuclear fissions.

He and the Americans had explained all this to him in terms of millions of degrees of heat and millionths of seconds of time and, since neither is intelligible to the lay mind, Cheshire had not really comprehended at all. He merely expected a mighty explosion of an unusual kind but nothing to be apprehensive about.

Why should he be apprehensive? He had personally witnessed, and largely been responsible for, the two most fantastic chemical explosions of the war so far. He had seen the destruction of the naval ammunition dump at Wilhelmshaven and the obliteration of the powder works at Bergerac. On both occasions the chemical explosion had been cataclysmic and exhilarating. They had set out to destroy and they had destroyed. Two vast, unprecedented, indescribably superb explosions they had been. No . . . after Wilhelmshaven and Bergerac, Nagasaki would not come as a surprise. Let the scientists talk theoretically of millions and millionths—he had *seen* destruction.

The time was drawing close now, the time for the dropping of the bomb. Broad daylight without a cloud in the sky: yet still they passed on their way unmolested. At four hundred miles an hour they approached the target. Silence, broken only by the whir of the compressor and the rush of conditioned-air, fell on the crew of the observing plane. He was warm, almost too warm. It was like sun-bathing on a ship, this war from the stratosphere.

They were very close to Nagasaki now—and the bomb in the first plane, the bomb they had assembled so urgently in the last two weeks, was even closer.

He smiled as he recollected the story told by the two American security men who had brought out the core of the bomb from the United States to the Mariana Islands in the Pacific.

They had carried it in a small box. Everywhere they went they carried it with them. When they landed in Honolulu they went to a restaurant for lunch and took their little box with them.

"Parcels in the cloakroom, if you don't mind, sir," the head-waiter had remonstrated.

"This parcel stays with us," they declared, and produced papers to prove it. Asked what the box contained, they replied: "Shaving tackle," and finished their meal in enigmatic silence.

Funny little parcel to be the product of so much research by Americans and Britons in the desert of New Mexico. Men like Sir James Chadwick and Dr. Penney. Obviously they hoped, in their dispassionately academic fashion, for big things from it. Millions of degrees heat in millionths of second's time. Well . . . they would see what they would see.

They were all excited now. Cheshire and the crew with the exhilarating excitement of war and the power to destroy: the scientists with the intellectual excitement of endless theorizing and research now about to reach its fruition. They were vastly different forms of excitement—the one, youthful, vigorous, utterly human and understandable: the other, aged, calculating and cold. The order came to don their thick welders' glasses. The moment of history had arrived.

When he put his glasses on, Cheshire was disconcerted and not a little annoyed to find that he could not see outside at all. Dr. Penney was more patient. He knew what would follow, what they would see soon. He even knew what the people of Nagasaki would see soon—a brilliant flash in the sky that would sear eyeballs into instant blindness, a haze of rapidly onrushing and darkening white smoke, an instant's sound of roaring accompanied by the oppression of wind and heat . . . then oblivion. So, calmly, the scientist waited.

But Cheshire fidgeted, mentally and physically. How could any man-made flash, twenty miles away, be so menacing as to demand glasses through which now, in broad daylight, he could hardly see at all? How could . . .?

It was the bomb itself that answered all his questions for him. Without warning, the warm sunlit interior of his cockpit was suffused with a vicious, flaring brightness, stronger even than that of the sun itself. Every detail of the plane's interior now stood out, through his welder's glasses, in sharp-edged clarity. Swiftly he turned his head to the source of this unspeakable light and was appalled.

Over Nagasaki was a ball of fire rocketing upwards ascending five times as fast as even the new jet aeroplanes could fly—a ball of fire miles across, billowing and malignant

Attached to it was a tail, a tail of smoke and vapour and destruction which, it seemed, had torn off the very crust of the earth itself.

With turbulent writhings the fire-ball darkened, losing its original incandescent glare, and changed itself into a vast, luminous cloud—a foul cloud, evilly alive, living and feeding through its tail on the death that lay below. This, then, was the ultimate fruit of nuclear physics and man's inventiveness, a mushroom whose belly grew bloated on the flash-burned flesh of those other men who had lived below, a sort of vicarious cannibalism.

There was something so horrific in the sight that no explosion at Wilhelmshaven or Bergerac could make it even faintly comprehensible. Those other scenes of destruction had been merely what one would expect when thousands of tons of munitions, or the manufacturing source of supersensitive high-explosive, were accurately bombed. But Nagasaki was something no ordinary man, not even a man briefed in advance by the cleverest scientists, could ever anticipate. It was a flash and a blast that at one and the same time made warfare seem incredible and civilization futile.

The Group Captain who flew back from Japan to the Marianas, after four hours of observation, was a changed man. No longer did he notice the unwonted warmth and silence of the American plane. The height at which they flew and the comfort in which they travelled were now unimportant to him who hated the one and had for years, in cold, noisy Lancasters and Halifaxes, been accustomed to the other.

He was probably the man who could claim personally to be responsible for more destruction to enemy property than any other in the war. Fittingly he had climaxed his battle career by attending the military explosion of the greatest bomb man had ever invented. Yet now, for the first time, he did not exult in his achievement, felt no elation. He knew only one thing at this moment, that the world must look to something else in the future than wars and nuclear physics whereby to sustain itself.

If Hiroshima and Nagasaki were our civilization's supreme moment of history, they were equally, to Leonard Cheshire, V.C., his personal moment of destiny.

Chapter Two

STOWE AND POTSDAM

THE YOUTHFUL CHESHIRE gave no indication to his family, or, later, to his school, of the distinction he was to achieve by the time he was twenty-six.

He was born in Chester in September 1917, when tanks, U-boats and poison gas were euphemistically regarded as the ultimate horrors of modern warfare. Wars have improved considerably since then, and to their improvement the infant Leonard was himself to make handsome contributions.

He did not remain long in the county whose name he bore. "We left Chester when he was one year old," his father explained. "We haven't lived there since." He went on to add: "Actually we are a Cheshire family in fact as well as name. My family hails from Hartford in the Northwich area."

They are a long-established legal family, the Cheshires. Great-grandfather Christopher was a solicitor and registrar to the Court at Northwich: his son Walter succeeded him: Leonard's own father, Dr. G. C. Cheshire, has attained the highest legal academic laurels and produced classic text-books on the Law of Property.

As a child, it seemed that the young Leonard was not obsessed with any vaunting ambitions for greatness.

"What do you want to be?" he was asked.

"Just an ordinary man," he replied modestly, and then explained, "like my father."

From this remark two equally justifiable conclusions can

be drawn. First, that Cheshire, even in those days, was excessively modest: second, that, again even in those days, he displayed that fiendish sense of irony and capacity for under-statement which distinguish his conversation now. Because the father whose "ordinary" footsteps he so placidly stated he wished to follow was in fact to become Bursar of an Oxford College and a most distinguished Vinerian Professor of Law!

At the age of fourteen Leonard obtained a scholarship from the Dragon School at Oxford to enter the recently founded Public School of Stowe.

This school was originally the fine Adam country house which had been the seat of the Dukes of Buckingham and Chandos—local landowners who had been recommended for elevation to the peerage by a grateful William Pitt, first Earl of Chatham.

Both the north and south fronts of the main building have tremendous Grecian porticoes which quite obscure the en-trance to the house: the main hall has a superb Bertoli ceiling: many of the dormitories are vast, vaulted chambers.

The south front looks down twenty-five stone steps, across a glorious stretch of grass, to a miniature *Arc de Triomphe* about half a mile distant, through which, on a clear day, Buckingham itself can be seen.

It was into these classic surroundings that, in 1923, the first headmaster, Roxburghe, brought his nucleus of new boys. Moulding the dignified character of the building to the customary revolting behaviour of small boys, and that of the revolting small boys to the splendours of their surroundings, Roxburghe, in a few short years, achieved the miracle of creat-ing a first-class public school. He burnt himself out com-pletely doing so and had to retire finally through utter nervous exhaustion.

It was, then, to this school that Leonard Cheshire came in 1932. Dwarfed by the Grecian porticoes on the outside of the building, he vanished humbly through the main porchway. He was a small boy for his age and this general air of architectural vastness and grandeur did nothing to improve his morale.

He was assigned to one of the new wings specially added to accommodate schoolboys—Chatham House. Typically, Cheshire never allowed this fact to affect his subsequent choice of career. Though it would have been splendidly symbolic for anyone who decided to enter either politics or the Navy, this latest addition to the members of Stowe was to choose, as his first serious vocation, the Royal Air Force at war. For the moment, though, all that lay in the future.

Duly impressed by the stately drive that led up to the school, by the grandiose architecture of the place, by its generous sprinkling of pavilions, follies and statues, and most of all by his own utter insignificance as a "new boy," the young Leonard set about making himself unobtrusively at home.

Quickly he settled down. He played every game it was possible to play (rugby, tennis, squash, fives, soccer, hockey and cricket), thereby placating the great public school gods, and even indulged, with furious loyalty, in cross-country running. "Though why," he says now, "I can't imagine. I know I never won and I always felt terrible the next day."

The headmaster's secretary, Mr. Lucas, says: "I remember him very well for his love of tennis and athletics." The first of these alleged loves Cheshire will unhesitatingly acknowledge: but the second was no true love at all—rather the attitude of a polite, small boy who, at a school ball, dutifully dances with an habitual "wallflower."

"I recall him as a short, slim, quiet boy," Lucas continued. It is strange that almost everyone remembers Cheshire as "short, slim and quiet." Nowadays the description is qualified slightly—"short, slim, quiet . . . and a V.C." But there is more to him than that.

Lucas taught Cheshire to play tennis, a game at which he was to excel. He played an all-court game, using sound ground strokes and a keen, anticipatory brain to make the opening which left him a kill at the net. The game had a great significance for him, especially the cunning cut and thrust of doubles, and at anything that has significance for him he has always done extremely well.

About rugby football he is not so enthusiastic. He played it assiduously, and without any spectacular success, right through his school days. He abandoned it finally and without a trace of grief when he entered the less conventional environment of Oxford.

"As a matter of fact," declares this five-times decorated war hero, "I was a little frightened of football—always seemed a bit rough." In short, he saw very little sense, or future, in spending every winter, as scrum half, flat on his face in the mud under the attacking bodies of two evilly-disposed enemy breakaways. "Much preferred tennis," he admits with a charming smile, and no shame at all.

It was a rugby forward of huge proportions who was Leonard's best friend at Stowe, one J. T. McKay Anderson, who subsequently, with the Argylls at Longstop Hill, was to win a Victoria Cross. This friendship and a later one with Jack Randle at Oxford raise the query as to whether there is a certain imperceptible quality of innate heroism in young men which can attract equals to equals within a tiny, select circle, for Randle also won a Victoria Cross, and so did Randle's brother-in-law.

It may be claimed that *all* the Argylls invariably fight as if each were determined to win a V.C.: or that any two young men who would go down on their knees, as did Cheshire and Randle at the time of the Munich crisis in 1938, and *pray* for war will inevitably gain this high distinction. The cold, hard fact remains, however, that all three have been thus decorated and that Cheshire enjoyed the closest friendship of the other two. He alone, today, survives.

Actually it was on April 23rd, 1943, that Anderson won his V.C., having only a month earlier earned a D.S.O. in North Africa.

The war had by then reached Tunisia. A vital objective assigned to Princess Louise's Argyll and Sutherland Highlanders was Longstop Hill. As a General, also named Anderson, commented: "That was the one place, above all, in Tunisia, we just had to have."

It was to be taken in two assaults and it seems that the hill's strategic importance had not escaped the notice of the Germans for it was held in tremendous strength.

By the time the Argylls had reached their first objective, Captain Anderson alone (of the C.O., the Adjutant, the Intelligence Officer and all the Company Commanders) survived. Knowing that if the second objective, the peak of the hill itself, was not captured the entire First Army would be held up, he assumed command of the battalion, reorganized it and himself led the next assault.

The enemy were determined and their cleverly concealed machine guns and mortars wrought heavy casualties on the attacking Scots as they advanced up an open slope. With most of his men pinned down or dead, Anderson reached the hill-top with four junior officers and less than forty Other Ranks.

Limping badly from a leg wound, he nevertheless personally led the attacks on three machine-gun posts and a gun-pit containing four mortars. Each time he was first into the enemy nest. He and his small band captured two hundred of the enemy and made it possible for the rest of the regiment to advance to the peak and take up their positions.

As he lay panting and bleeding from his exertions, the position now secure, a war correspondent asked him how on earth they had made it when so many others had failed.

"I don't know," Anderson replied. "I think we got angry suddenly—at the hill and the Germans and everything. Seemed as if everyone suddenly said, 'Oh, hell, let's finish this bloody thing.'"

Looking back in his mind on the tumult of machine-gun fire which was more vicious and sustained than anything he had ever heard before, even in Tunisia, and on the foam of blue-grey smoke and brown dust which rose in an unbroken wave all along the hillside, the correspondent began to understand the wild Gaelic respect in which the Argylls held their new leader.

When everyone else had been brought to earth, if not by wounds then by exhaustion, "we all got so bloody tired," one officer explained, Anderson had charged on. So, at the age of twenty-five, he won the highest award a soldier can gain. Before he could be invested with it, he was killed on the battlefield of Italy.

So much for Anderson's story: but at this moment Leonard Cheshire is sixteen years old and still at school.

In his second year at Stowe his brother Christopher came to join him. Christopher was fair-haired, blue-eyed and a family favourite. No one contributed more to this favouritism than elder brother Leonard. They were very close, and Cheshire, for years, spent a lot of his time protectively worrying about the other lad, who probably, to gather from his war record, did not need such protection anyway.

"Look after him," Cheshire requested of Lucas, as the master was about to give Christopher his first tennis lesson, "he's got a bad leg, you know."

Probably nothing built up more strongly the emotional background of fraternal protectiveness in their relationship than this bad leg. Like most small boys, young Leonard had very little patience with sickness. Christopher, who suffered from the painful naggings of osteomyelitis, slept beside Leonard and frequently groaned as the darting pain of the bone that rotted in his leg struck him. Typically, as an older brother, Leonard considered that most, if not all, of this embarrassing noise was quite unnecessary.

"Shut up," he demanded. "There's nothing the matter really. And you're keeping me awake."

"I was very fed up," he explained many years later. "But that same night they whipped him off to hospital and he was on the operating-table for over four hours. I felt very guilty about that for years."

And so, to compensate for this sense of guilt, he became more than normally thoughtful for and protective towards his brother. Right through Oxford and into the war this trait persisted. He was to take pleasure in the fact that he and Christopher played in the same College tennis team: he was to be proud that he and Christopher, on three or four occasions, were together over the same target in Germany: and he still glows far more readily over Christopher's war record than he does over his own.

"Did you hit your target tonight?" he was asked once.

"No, too much cloud."

"Your brother did," he was told, goadingly.

"Did he?" Cheshire enthused. "Good show."

Today, inevitably, the relationship is not so close. With many of his brother's notions Christopher now disagrees, but a strong affection still remains.

The years at school passed. "He was very quiet here," Lucas comments. "It was only at Oxford that he broke out a little." The subject of these remarks puts the case rather differently.

"I worked rather hard at school. Was quite good at languages—and terrible at maths. It was at Oxford that I started NOT to work." In any event it seems to be agreed by all concerned that he was conscientious, a good Prefect and House Captain, and, by the time he left Stowe, most popular with his fellow pupils.

"A good worker," his Greek and Latin Master says of him. "Not outstanding: but a good, average chap."

One can ask no better of the English educational system than to emerge from it classified as "a good average chap." To be more is to be suspect: to be less is to be a dolt—but to be a good average chap leaves the field wide open to becoming anything from a remittance man in Australia to the Prime Minister himself.

1935 arrived, and with it came Cheshire's Higher Certificate in Classics. He had one more term to do at school. Instead, his father suggested that a few months on the Continent would do him no harm. Through a family friend it was planned that he should spend this period in the household of an Admiral von Reuter, who lived in Potsdam.

"I'm sure my housemaster was most relieved that I left early," Cheshire remarks. "I was a bit of a trial for him . . . Can't remember exactly how, but I distinctly remember being one." Even if he can't remember, and the Housemaster will not say, it is quite possible that this was so, for his record today, during the war and at Oxford, has never displayed an over-zealous regard for authority, so why should we suspect that he had it then?

In any event, slim, dark-haired, heavy-browed, his face triangular and broodingly sensitive, but lightened by a frequent wide smile of sheer mischief and joy, the young English boy now packed up and went to live in Germany.

This was late 1935, when Hitler was really beginning to hit his form. But upon the youthful Cheshire neither Hitlerism, Germans nor Germany made any profound effect. He returned in 1936 aware of no great military menace, though he was not unintelligent. He perceived no hideous threat of aggression, though he is acutely perceptive. He sensed no rottenness of political morality, though he is far from insensitive. Years later, in 1949, he was to warn an audience to whom he lectured in Britain:

"There are dangerous undercurrents in Germany. They tricked me in 1935: they tricked me in 1946. They must not trick us again."

Perhaps, though, it was not so much that he was tricked as that he was Anglo-Saxon, one hundred per cent Anglo-Saxon, and fully armed with all the Briton's stolid obtuseness and exquisitely polite indifference to anything that happens beyond the English Channel. As Uncle Matthew, in one of Nancy Mitford's novels, put it:

"Frogs are slightly better than Huns or Wops, but abroad is unutterably bloody and foreigners are fiends." This was a thoroughly English sentiment in the 1920's and a modified version of it inevitably fell upon all those who, in 1935, were just leaving school as "good average chaps."

So, securely swaddled in the great English truth that "Being abroad is unutterably bloody and all foreigners are fiends," the seventeen-year-old Cheshire saw nothing untoward in the von Reuter household, whose three sons were fervent Nationalists, nor in Berlin itself, which was a hotbed of military parades and speech-making.

Admiral von Reuter of Potsdam was best known and admired in Germany for what other nations would regard as a supreme failure. He it was who ordered the German fleet to scuttle itself in Scapa Flow after the Reich's surrender in 1918. Now the Admiral is completely forgotten in the light of a recent, even more humiliating national defeat and Potsdam itself is notable for a far more disastrous failure. In 1935, however, the Admiral was still a person of some consequence.

He was not a Party member ("too old—the Nazis had very little use for members who were too old for some form of active service," explains Cheshire cynically) but he thoroughly approved his sons' membership and also all things military.

"Only five per cent of mankind is worth keeping," he told Cheshire then. "The rest should be put down. War is a good way of getting rid of the rabble." His schoolboy guest looked shocked. He had no aversion at all to war, indeed it sounded most exciting, but he did not consider ninety-five per cent of his fellow-men as rabble to be put down by its waging.

"Don't you agree?" demanded the Admiral.

"No, sir," replied the English boy, "I don't."

The Admiral was furious at this failure to agree and at such queasy soft-heartedness. As the Führer had so often said, the English were decadent.

"He was a hard old devil," Cheshire relates, without a trace of malice. "I remember he named all his sons after battleships he had commanded at one time or another. Treated them shockingly. On the other hand, he had a very nice side and I liked him."

On one occasion, at the time of the Olympic Games in Berlin, the eldest of the von Reuter boys, who had somehow managed to secure a ticket to these games, arrived late to dinner.

"Give me your ticket," the outraged father demanded. Obediently his son handed it over, though it was as hard to come by as an audience with Hitler himself and twice as valuable as its weight in gold. Irritably the Admiral tore it in half and flung the two pieces under the table: parental authority was thus retained and his sons spared the hideous fate of joining the undisciplined rabble.

By all these displays of force, however, the English schoolboy remained serenely untouched. A monster military parade was being held in Berlin and to this, the Admiral decreed, Leonard should go. He could not very well march in it, as the three von Reuter boys were doing, therefore he should watch it. With deceptive mildness Cheshire agreed. He, the Admiral and the Admiral's wife took their places together in a crowd which seethed with excitement and fervour. The shameful days of Versailles were past and all of Germany rejoiced, for here, in this mighty parade of armour, was the proof of it.

As the first tanks rumbled past, as the first close-packed, goose-stepping soldiers came into sight, there came a huge roar from every throat and every arm stretched outwards, febrile and fanatical, in the salute of Hitler's Third Reich. Every arm, that is, except Leonard Cheshire's. He stood silent and unresponsive and saluted in no way at all.

Gruffly the Admiral chided him. Cheshire did not accept the rebuke. The Admiral's wife looked at him pleadingly. It was not good, even in 1935, to be seen in the company of one who displayed no enthusiasm for the Party. Still Cheshire would not cheer or salute.

The crowd began to mutter antagonistically but the English schoolboy was unmoved by mob displeasure. All he knew was that he had waited five hours for this accursed parade and that, long before it arrived, he had got very, very bored. The whole thing, to him, reeked of humourless "square bashing," and after five hours of boredom he was certainly not going to participate. The only concession he would make, in his own mind, was to admit that the Germans *did* seem to have a lot of tanks.

"Probably that's because you very seldom see them at home though," he told himself, and dismissed the thought.

So he stood, his serious face unlit by his usual smile, his heavy eyebrows knitted together with bored irritability, his manner remote, his bearing polite but limp and unenthusiastic. Nothing, not the Admiral, Frau von Reuter nor the mutterings of the crowd around could change him.

Since nothing is more difficult to oppose than the will of

an angry mob and since this was a mob almost frenzied with
the fanaticism of adults who have lost all sense of proportion
(whilst Cheshire was only a lad too young yet to have acquired
one), his stolid refusal to salute can probably be taken to
indicate a high degree of innate moral and physical courage.
Certainly it is ironic to reflect what trouble and damage to
their beloved Fatherland that gathering could have saved themselves had they annihilated the youngster then and there rather
than merely shout at him and let him live to raid Europe on
exactly one hundred occasions later on.

Soon after this episode Cheshire left the von Reuter household and took up residence with a family called Kelsch. They,
too, had three sons.

The eldest of these, Hans, had a passion for speed—which
passion he expressed in the possession of a very powerful
motor-bike and also by attendance at every possible race-car
meeting. Though not greatly enamoured of the motor-bike
which he found much too dangerous, Cheshire became instantly infected by the other lad's passion for speed. In the company of Hans he saw all the greatest Continental drivers and his
only ambition in life grew to be not Law at Oxford, not being
"an ordinary man like my father," not learning German,
though he now spoke it quite proficiently, but driving a very
fast car round a very curved track and joggling the steering
wheel like the race stars did.

And so came the time for him to leave Germany and go
home, soon to enter Oxford. Naturally, he had matured a
little in experience: but in temperament, if anything, he had
become more boyish and less restrained.

Perhaps, had he known that before five years were out he
was to bomb Berlin time after time, he would have departed
more soberly. Perhaps, had he known that the Admiral's war
to put down the ninety-five per cent rabble would, in the
process, kill all the Admiral's sons, he would have left

them a little more sentimentally. Perhaps, had he known that one Kelsch boy was to be killed over Russia, another shot down over England and only the third to survive unscathed, he would have remembered them for something else than an introduction to Continental car racing.

But he knew none of this. All he knew was that he was going home, and thence to Oxford to study, in the family tradition, Law. He was not sorry to leave Germany and he never suspected for one minute that he would revisit it so soon or under such curiously inhospitable conditions.

Chapter Three

THE STRAW MEN

CHESHIRE'S famous last words about his under-graduate career, which began in 1936, are: "It was at Oxford I started *not* to work." Certainly all the facts bear out this frank assessment.

He arrived quietly at Merton, but in a very short time learned the ropes and then blossomed out spectacularly with four suits, which was unusual, and a supercharged Alfa Romeo, which was forbidden. A blue blazer and flannels were the regulation outfit of most college residents: and the college regulation in respect of cars was that they should be owned by undergraduates in their third year or above only. Cheshire had the suits kept in order by an Oxford tailor and the car he hid from the eagle eyes of authority in devious back streets and lanes of the noble university city.

The desire for a fast car of his own had been born in Germany as he watched Continental aces racing one another. This desire had been fostered by a slight difference of opinion with his father on the day of his return from Europe.

His father had met him when he landed in England and to-gether they drove home to Abingdon. Cheshire junior sat in the driver's seat and, with all the verve and cocksureness of an eighteen-year-old, promptly put into effect the frantic joggling motions of all racing drivers when they steer. Cheshire senior observed this performance with a disapprovingly judicial eye for some miles and then demanded, with that legal precision which has made his text-books so famous, was it all necessary?

Confronted with the irrefutable proposition that driving a speed car on a race track at ninety miles an hour is rather different from driving the family Austin on an English highway at forty, Leonard was compelled to agree that his antics were *not* necessary. But he could barely contain his impatience for the day when he would own a vehicle of sufficient power, speed and menace to make it so. Hence, at Oxford, the supercharged and illicit Alfa Romeo.

The rash seeds of his independence, so richly sown in Germany, now swiftly grew into handsome weeds of folly at Oxford. Gone was the serious-minded schoolboy who studied as hard as he was expected to and conscientiously played games whether he liked them or not. In his place stood an immature young man whose only obsession was to live excitingly and whose greatest horror was work. As for sport—football was too rough and rowing too cold. He played only tennis. Any intention he may ever have entertained as a boy of going far in the profession of Law was now burned out of him by his feverish desire for the spectacular.

Not that this was surprising. Cheshire was of that generation whose German contemporaries had cold-bloodedly, as thirteen and fourteen-year-olds, gone into the woods and hanged themselves. He was of the generation that had caught childhood glances of the reckless Twenties. Contemporary literature in his youth was cynical, disillusioned and atheistic: the theatre was brittle and empty of thought, for all its drawing-room epigrams.

Nor was this all in Cheshire's generation. The Depression years were their teen-age years: the Spanish Civil War tore their loyalties to shreds: the Abdication rocked their sense of national immutability: British Fascists praised Hitler whilst Hitler threatened Britain.

For Cheshire's generation these late 1930's were years that had killed optimism. Gone was the solidity of Victorian days; gone the rich-living of Edwardian days. Grandfather had found his excitement in big game hunting. Incomes were too small now in families like Cheshire's to hunt big game. Father had found his excitement in the birth and development of the internal combustion engine and exploration by air. But by 1938 all the oceans had been flown: cars had been driven as fast as they would ever move and planes piloted as swiftly as they could fly—or so it seemed.

There was no excitement, no easy wealth, no inviolate social security of caste and prosperity; there was no faith and no future. Cheshire's post-war generation were indeed lost. Their heritage was waste land. Why not then taste the stray fruits of disenchantment?

"We are the hollow men," wrote T. S. Eliot, "the straw men." Their environment was the conflict of loyalties of the Spanish Civil War, the conflict of the viewpoints of Mosley, Churchill, Hitler and Chamberlain. Their background was the disaster of war and depression; their future, helpless extinction. Everyone told them so.

> "That is the way the world ends
> Not with a bang, but a whimper."

Again Eliot spoke hopelessly for them all.

And here, in the midst of all this, stood young Cheshire, round-faced, serious and intelligent enough to sense that his school classification of a "good average chap" did him no justice in comparison with the hefty full-back who passed as "brilliant". Sensitive enough to perceive the future contradictions of the adult world that controlled him. But not yet authoritative enough, at eighteen, to defy and change the madness he inherited.

And he lived, in college, in a contradictory environment that made this madness doubly lunatic. Whilst Hitler rampaged and the world crumbled, he dined graciously in Hall and then withdrew to the Buttery to drink ale on unlimited credit.

Whilst Storm Troopers marched and drilled, he and his fellow undergraduates dressed in elegant flannels and punted their lady friends on the river. They lounged in the Junior Common Room drinking tea, eating chocolate éclairs and reading the glossies with a bored eye and a blasé mind. They were expected to live without a thought in their heads except Rags and bonfires on Guy Fawkes night. All this was tradition which had to be upheld; although the past from which it stemmed was crumbling before their eyes.

The only laws that truly affected them were the rules of "sconcing," which covered dining etiquette: the only possible means of asserting one's own personality in this quagmire of pessimism was to reject all other laws and conventions and to strike out violently on one's own.

Faced with the prospect of disaster promised to them by all, from the dons, who talked over their mellow port in the sanctified atmosphere of the Senior Common Room, to the politicians who raved on their soap boxes, Cheshire and his colleagues arrived at a very natural youthful decision. If disaster were to be theirs, at least it would be of their own making.

Thus, in the soft surroundings of Oxford, all pale sun and cool shade, ancient stone, staunch tradition and doomed youth in flannels, Cheshire and his friends ran riot. If there was trouble ahead, Cheshire maintained, one did much better to go out and meet it. It was a philosophy he was eventually to take with him to the war and one that saved him, a thousand times, from being afraid.

"I must have caused Father lots of headaches," he murmurs

apologetically, recalling all his outrages upon the authorities of Oxford, of whom Dr. Cheshire was one. "He was very good. Never said anything," and then, not very repentantly, "poor Father!"

His craving for excitement led to innumerable escapades, the craziest of which, undoubtedly, was the "car" game he played regularly with Jack Randle.

They would stand on the kerb, these two youngsters, and wait for cars to approach. Then, at the last second, they would dash out across the path of the oncoming vehicle. The competition was to see who could cut it finest across the bows of Oxford's horrified motorists. It was not till Leonard lost his shoe, pinned by its sole under the front tyre of one of these speeding cars, that they decided to give this entrancing sport away.

"The bloke got out of his car very annoyed and said he could easily have killed me and he'd had half a mind to knock me down. We packed it in."

Thenceforward they placated their insatiable thirst for adventure by driving often to London and going to "the dogs."

"Don't think I ever made any money," Cheshire relates, "but I met quite a lot of toughs and gaol-birds, and that was interesting."

After "the dogs" they would drink until three in the morning, roar back to Oxford in the Alfa Romeo (it was a point of honour to complete the journey in under an hour), hide the car, climb the two walls of Merton, one fiercely spiked, and retire to bed till seven when the scout, Bert Gardner, would attempt to rouse them.

"Come on now, Mr. Cheshire," Bert would say. "Seven o'clock. Time to get up." Mr. Cheshire would open one eye, shut it and say not a word.

But Bert had been looking after young gentlemen like

Cheshire for years. He knew their ways, and how to deal with them, perfectly. He even knew exactly what sort of a pass they would achieve in their examinations.

"You'll get a Second," he told an unenthusiastic Cheshire. "And he did," he reports now, triumphantly.

For the moment, though, Bert is confronted with a somnolent and reluctant young gentleman, and seven others like him still to be roused, whom it is his difficult duty to get out of bed and down to roll-call by eight o'clock.

He had long since learnt that, though the abuse hurled at his devoted head for not letting them sleep on was appalling, it was as nothing compared to that which befell him if he did not rouse them and they were fined a pound for missing roll-call in consequence.

So Bert stands his ground and stolidly declares: "I'm not going till you've answered me."

"Most days," according to the scout, "Mr. Cheshire used to get up at the very last second, fling on his clothes and hurl himself down the stairs—and woe betide anyone coming up, they'd be thrown clear out of the way."

Term after term, life continued merrily. Cheshire would make himself tea in the morning and partake of a mild and restorative breakfast in his room. Occasionally he would tire of this solitary meal, though not enough to go down to the college breakfast, and would then make a party of it with four or five others. Defying the havoc it wrought upon a stomach well lined with last night's alcohol, they would all partake of grape fruit, porridge, kidneys and bacon and, finally, sausages.

From here it was but a short step to luncheon parties. These Cheshire dispensed on a grand scale. Sherry and a barrel of beer, dozens of oysters, fish, meat, game, sweet, cheese and coffee.

"Did themselves well," is Bert's opinion. "Lady friends,

too, he had at these luncheons. Not always the same lady either. Seemed to be quite a few of them—*and* pretty."

And then, at night, late and companionably, they would meet in one another's rooms, small groups of two or three or four—groups that swelled and dwindled casually as men dropped in, chatted and then wandered off, to their books, or another room, or to bed. They would sit on the table, the chairs, the bed and the floor. They would discuss Schopenhauer and women, politics and athletics: they would listen conscientiously to Brahms or jazz or whatever was fashionable. Then, full of coffee and chocolate biscuits and good company, they would break up the party and go contentedly to sleep. They had done no work but they had enjoyed themselves enormously.

When the exams came, smitten by conscience, Cheshire would slave for about three weeks and pass creditably enough, though he remembered nothing of what he had crammed ten minutes after each paper was completed.

Visits to "the dogs," cakes baked by his mother and sent to him from home, late nights, hard drinking, fast driving, the endless scaling of college walls and tennis were the gaudy fabric of Cheshire's undergraduate days. There was also constant irritation from an overseas student who slept in the room below him.

He disliked the man so heartily, not because he was a foreigner but because he was always drunk. He drank not for pleasure or to be sociable but merely to get helplessly intoxicated. He was the original inspiration of all those words like "blind," "plastered," "pie-eyed" and "stinking." And always he seemed to be returning to college just as Cheshire and his colleagues were doing so in the early hours of the morning, so that it became their hated duty to lug him over both walls with them.

Cheshire's aversion to the drunkard reached its peak when,

as they were dragging his inert corpse over the spiked wall one night, he came violently to life.

"Lashed out with his fists and feet and scattered us all over the shop," Cheshire reports, his face screwed up with distaste. "Very boring."

Inspired both by compassion and by his fatal aversion to being unpleasant to anyone, Cheshire would send a bottle of beer down, at breakfast-time, to the room below his own on the dubious principle of "a hair of the dog that bit you." Then, as now, he could never completely show dislike for anyone.

He decided one day to revisit Stowe. The decision sprang equally from an old boy's desire to see his ex-masters from a non-pupil's status, and from a young man's desire to show off in his car. He took with him a German fellow student.

At Stowe they had a pleasant afternoon with Mr. Lucas. They discussed tennis hopefuls at the school and Cheshire's own prospects of a Blue for the game at Oxford. Then came the time to leave and Lucas escorted the two young men out to the drive.

This drive was curved, gravelled and tempting. Moreover it passed the edge of the cricket field and on that edge, curiously surveying the exalted undergraduate in his magnificent sports car, stood a group of admiring schoolboys. Even if they were *not* admiring, the youthful Cheshire at once determined that they should be.

Letting in the clutch and accelerating hard, he roared off down the drive and took the high-cambered bend at speed, waving good-bye with a nonchalant hand. Immediately his rear wheels slid wildly and he found himself completely out of control.

Twice he skidded round, then plunged briskly through a sight-screen on to the cricket field and finally, abruptly, capsized on to his side. Through a chaos of shattered white lattice-work and the bent remains of his Alfa Romeo, he stepped out on to the grass. He was greeted with howls of schoolboy laughter.

"Very humiliating," he said. "Also it cost me twenty-two pounds for the sight-screen and took me hours to get the car going again."

His German passenger crawled stolidly out of his seat, gave Cheshire a glare of concentrated Teutonic hatred and then announced coldly: "Thank you."

Mrs. Cheshire, upon hearing of this incident, promptly had words with Mr. Lucas.

"Couldn't you," she asked, "somehow wean him away from all those fast and peculiar cars? They're so dangerous," she explained. Mrs. Cheshire, wholly delightful, the best possible mother, a superb cooker of cakes and a fanatical gardener, never understood how anyone, least of all a son of hers, could be so crazy about speed.

If only she had known it, much worse was to come. No longer able fully to satisfy his craving for excitement by driving his supercharged sports car, Cheshire, in his second year at college, decided to learn to fly.

"Nothing like it," he vowed, and so took the first positive step in the long road that has led him to the position he holds today.

Cheshire joined the Oxford University Air Squadron and trained happily with it twice a week for the rest of his undergraduate career. On each visit he would fly for three-quarters of an hour, mostly just "circuits and bumps," and never once did he display any particular genius in aeronautics.

"I wasn't a good pilot," he confesses frankly. "Not at all. Never have been."

He secured only an average pass-out and, except for one isolated occasion, never caused his instructor to entertain the smallest hopes for him; and even that occasion depended entirely for its effectiveness upon a cold-blooded fraud.

He was on an instrument flight, a form of highly calculated and mathematical flying which he loathed. Actually the only kind of flying he really enjoyed was low flying. He was afraid of heights! And one of his favourite landmarks was a pub standing on its own near the squadron's low-flying area. So it happened that on this instrument flight, always above cloud, the earth lost and invisible, the instructor suddenly asked him where he was.

Expected to provide the answer to this unpleasantly penetrating question by computing all the distances he had covered and the bearings he had taken (something almost beyond his powers), he glanced frantically round, seeking inspiration. And at that moment, there, below him, revealed briefly by a gap in the clouds, he saw his pub.

"Near our low-flying area," Cheshire announced confidently, thereby stunning the instructor, who would never have believed that any of his pupils could have estimated his position so swiftly and with such complete accuracy.

But if his flying was nothing out of the ordinary ("he was never recognized as a great pilot when he was in the University squadron," his ex-instructor admits with some bewilderment), his knowledge of how planes flew, of their airframes and engines, was very sound indeed. This again was a quality he was to take with him to the war. Every aircraft he has ever flown he has compelled himself mercilessly to know as intimately as a man knows the whiskers in his own repulsive morning beard.

In 1937 he was photographed with his contemporaries in front of a Hawker Hart. A wistful young man, short and shy-looking, strange material for one of the war's most efficient and determined destroyers. On another occasion he was photographed alone: and here he looks even more diffident and unforceful. Both these photographs and his Victoria Cross citation now occupy a place of honour in the squadron's club-room.

But in 1938 Victoria Crosses and citations—or anything serious for that matter—seemed supremely remote to any of the squadron's members, and to none more so than Leonard. He was much too busy working on his car and devising means of not studying to worry about anything else, except, perhaps, a steady stream of remarkable blondes who have left a far stronger impression on the memory of the club than Cheshire's flying ever did.

"He used to change his cars often," ex-Squadron Leader Acres said. "Girls, too, for that matter." And on one unforgettable occasion, when he was repairing an old Austin Seven, Cheshire's legs and another pair of legs were seen to be protruding from under the chassis. When the bodies emerged it was found that the second pair of legs belonged to a gorgeous flaxen-haired Scandinavian girl whom Cheshire had persuaded, quite effortlessly, to help him with the greasing.

"No one else could've done it," Acres muttered with reluctant praise. Yet here again is a quality which, apparently developed early, Cheshire has taken all through his life with him. To a quite fantastic degree people "do things for him." But more of that later.

The change of car, from the Alfa Romeo his mother dreaded so much to others less powerful, was a concession he made to family pressure. Or that is what he would have had them think. Actually the Romeo was proving too much for his allowance and in any event he now preferred flying. So, graciously, he intimated that he would be a good son and sell this racing monster, as Mother and Father asked—and thus made a virtue out of abandoning something that no longer greatly appealed to him anyway. Flying was now his passion though he preferred speed to altitude.

Indicative of this preference is an anecdote of this period.

One morning, very early, on his way to arouse his eight young gentlemen, Bert found Cheshire not in bed but clinging precariously to the ledge that leads round the college tower. Astounded equally by this unexpected sight and by the fact that Cheshire was already up, Bert reacted with typical English phlegm.

"Will you have a cup of tea, Mr. Cheshire?" he enquired solicitously, as if he were quite accustomed to finding his young gentlemen half way up towers in the early hours of the morning.

And Leonard, who had been stuck there for hours, terrified of the yawning chasm that lay below him, and unable to move, now snapped:

"Fetch a ladder and get me down."

"We did," concluded Bert. "He'd been there all night!"

Nowadays, Cheshire no longer recalls the incident but when it is suggested to him that probably he was so drunk at the time that he *couldn't* recall it he says: "More than possibly," and smiles a delightful though unrepentant grin. And he adds: "I've always been terrified of heights, even in a plane. Once we got up I always felt uncomfortable. Didn't like looking out over the side."

Strange then that at this time he should have planned to fly the Atlantic. This he proposed to do in one of Alan Cobham's old biplanes. He had no trouble persuading a business man to back the venture and even less trouble in persuading the boiler-man at Merton to join him as navigator.

"What on earth does *he* know about navigation?" his friends demanded explosively.

"Well, very little probably," Cheshire conceded, "but he's a jolly good bloke!" And though he now admits that they would quite certainly have crashed in the sea and died, there is still a gleam of nostalgia and disappointment in Cheshire's eye because the idea never came off.

Another idea, however, did come off. He was drinking one

night, in an Oxford pub, when he fell to discussing foreign travel with a truck-driver called Joseph Allen.

Allen maintained that travel to the Continent was for the idle rich only, the likes of young Cheshire, not himself. Cheshire disagreed strongly. He could easily, he maintained, get to Paris and back on the money he had in his pocket and anything he could earn on the way.

"Bet you can't," said Allen.

"Bet I can."

"How much have you got on you then?" Allen demanded suspiciously. Cheshire counted it out.

"Fifteen shillings."

"Bet you a pint you can't."

He landed at Dieppe at nine in the evening with a shilling in his pocket and not a care in the world.

Fifteen miles outside Dieppe he was stopped by an obvious tough who asked politely for a light and some money. Fingering his last shilling anxiously Cheshire assured the stranger, truthfully enough, that he had none. The stranger then demanded money. He was truculent, and big enough to be able to afford truculence.

Looking across at the dark woods that flanked each side of the road Cheshire realized that he was not in a healthy situation. His mind worked quickly.

"Well, what's *he* doing beside you anyway?" he demanded. The man turned his head to see who this intruder might be. Upon the jaw so exposed Cheshire landed a most ungallant haymaker and then fled.

"The worst part of the journey was the few miles that followed," he admits. "Kept looking back to see if he was after me."

For some hours more he walked along the road to Paris: but by then, in pouring rain, some of his youthful ardour had been dampened.

However, a car picked him up and he then spent a pleasant trip to within thirty miles of Paris in the company of an ex-Foreign Legion officer.

Cheshire told the officer the story of his wager and promptly gained employment digging that gentleman's garden. Though a singularly inept gardener, he was paid for his efforts and given a meal.

He next had a sleep in the Bois de Boulogne and then entered Paris in triumph. In the two days that followed he addressed the Anglo-American Press Club, delivered a broadcast and wrote of his experiences for the Paris papers.

He returned to England and Oxford, travelling first class all the way, on the proceeds of these his own unaided efforts. Four days after the wager had been made Cheshire collected his pint of beer from Allen.

"I thought that was the safest bet I ever made," the truck-driver mused. "Hell . . . Why didn't I go with him?"

No wonder all his contemporaries found him a bit of an enigma. Randle and he with their mad car game: the Atlantic project: the speedway race he entered when his car wouldn't start: the endless succession of gorgeous blondes: the contrast between him and Christopher who, since 1938, both at college and in the squadron, had impressed everyone with his quiet solidity: the diffident manner combined with a delightful wit and an ability to persuade anyone to do anything: the obviously good brain allied to an equally obvious playboy mentality: the Blue he should have got for tennis but didn't because he had torn his hand on the spikes of Merton's wall returning home early one morning: and finally, in late 1938, his genuine anguish that the Munich crisis ended not in war, but in Chamberlain's famous "Peace in our time."

President Benes of Czechoslovakia had resigned under pressure from his allies, and Hacha, on October 5th, had succeeded him. Cheshire's longed-for war, which had been so delightfully imminent, receded again into the background of an uneasy and tedious peace.

At this moment Cheshire's only consolation was that, however badly he felt about the failure of Europe's statesmen to present him with a war, Randle's disappointment was even deeper. Randle was almost distraught! A war would have provided them with exactly the sort of excitement they both craved *and* spared them the boredom of any further studies.

When the time came, they both enlisted promptly and joyously, Cheshire to achieve fame as Britain's greatest bomber pilot, Randle to die gloriously, if death in battle can ever be glorious, in Burma.

Since their University days were now drawing to a close, and because we shall not meet him again, it is perhaps fitting that we should here witness the circumstances that surrounded the death of one of Cheshire's greatest friends.

It was at the time of the Japanese thrust against India, when the enemy were being uncertainly held almost on the frontier itself. Randle's company were to counter-attack down a slope, across a stream, and up a hill. Randle had himself reconnoitred the Japanese position the night before and suffered a bullet in the leg in the process. Now came the attack.

Before they had reached the stream the Company Commander had been killed and Randle took over. In the stream itself a withering hail of machine-gun fire from a well-sited bunker up the opposite slope threatened to annihilate them all.

Randle at once attacked this position alone. He charged up the hill, was seen to be hit and then continue, to be hit again and still continue, and finally to throw his grenades inside the bunker. Just in case this should not be enough to silence the enemy, he then flung his own body over the aperture through which the machine gun fired. When the rest of the company reached him he was dead. He was awarded a posthumous V.C.

To revert back to early 1939, however, though the war for which each of these two young men so ardently prayed now approached with a steady and unfaltering tread, Cheshire's final examinations approached just as steadily, rather more rapidly and much more ominously.

Overcome with that remorse which only the undergraduate who has loafed unduly can experience, Cheshire now slaved to fulfil his rôle as son of one of Britain's greatest jurists. All day he studied, ignoring the allures of flying, motor-cars and blondes alike: all night he studied, sustaining himself on benzedrine and apparently driving out of his brain one long-cherished fact with every new one he assimilated.

After each of these bouts of work his scout would come in in the morning to find the room littered with notes in Cheshire's neat scrawl, with text-books that were small-printed and depressingly thick, and many empty coffee cups.

"You've been up late, Mr. Cheshire, working," he would reprove.

"Yes, Bert," Cheshire used to reply. "Sorry it's a bit of a mess."

The finals came and in a stupor of crammed learning, drugs and sleeplessness Cheshire wrote his papers. When the results came out he had got a Second. He, the son of Dr. Cheshire: he, of whom everyone, except Bert, had expected so much more.

"I suppose Father was disappointed," he comments, "but he didn't show it much."

It was to the inevitable war that he now looked for his salvation from a life of futility, from the practice of Law, from the nagging need for excitement which he seemed never able to satisfy.

He applied for a permanent commission in the R.A.F. and

six months later he was granted it. Then the longed-for conflict broke out. Ignoring the guarantee that Chamberlain had made to Poland following his occupation of Czechoslovakia, the Führer, having first secured a non-aggression pact with Russia, attacked the Poles, rejected a joint Anglo-French ultimatum and precipitated a war.

Cheshire sums it all up thus: "Had it not been for the war I might have done anything, and I don't mean anything much good. The war gave me a motive for life and an authority to live under. I was glad to get into it."

The days of his youthful irresponsibility were over. Now, at last, he was to grow up.

Chapter Four

BOMBER PILOT

WHEN HE APPLIED for his permanent commission,
Cheshire had hoped fervently that he would fly
single-seater fighters. He had worked hard on his
course and indulged in only one typical prank in that
time.

On this occasion, with three undergraduates, he had
climbed up into the Merton tower just before midnight. He
wanted to see what Oxford, the old familiar Oxford, looked
like in a blackout.

Somehow or other it came about that his three companions
left the tower, thinking he had already gone home, and
Cheshire was locked inside alone. It was only then, finding
himself in an eerie darkness from which he could not escape,
that Cheshire remembered that the tower was haunted, so
rumour had it, by the ghost of that great and gloomy medieval
philosopher, Duns Scotis.

Susceptible always to atmosphere, and innately a mystic
anyway, Cheshire at once found himself clammily apprehensive of a visit from the six-centuries-old ghost. He could talk
his way out of most things, yes: but out of the doom-laden and
haunted metaphysics of Duns Scotis, no!

It was icy cold and oppressively dark. And every quarter
of an hour the tower clock mechanism whirred, but remained
chimeless, tribute to the war. And every time the whirring
sounded, Cheshire looked round him anxiously. Was that

the clock or the approach of a long-dead medieval philospher? Only at dawn did he slide down on to the floor and, leaning against the stone wall, fall into a freezing sleep.

At the first sound of footsteps in the quadrangle below, he awoke and bellowed for help.

The key to the tower could not be found but the pilot who was so often to raid Germany without a qualm was in no mood any longer to remain in Merton's tower. He was retrieved at once with the aid of a rope and the college fire escape. Happily he returned to the more mundane atmosphere of his Training Unit. To his vast disgust, after having come out top of his class at his Officers' Training Unit at Hullavington, he was posted immediately to bombers, heavy bombers. His disgust quickly passed, however.

"Didn't take long to realize that heavy planes are the only comfortable means of transport," he explains. "I got rather dubious then about Spitfires and Hurricanes. Irresponsible contraptions. Two engines at least you need; preferably four!"

He was posted to 102 Squadron; Whitley bombers. He arrived there with fourteen hours' night and three hundred and eighty hours' day flying experience. He arrived, as he had both at Stowe and at Oxford, shy and diffident, a new boy. Unconfidently he surveyed his new colleagues, all of whom seemed hardened warriors to his tyro's eyes: and then, as he had always done in new surroundings, he settled down unobtrusively to learn the ropes.

He was to remain in 102 Squadron until midwinter of 1940–41. In that time he was to become one of a close circle of friends. These were the pilots, Lofty (his first captain), Willy, Lousy, Frammy, Desmond, Lib and Jimmy: and the aircrew, Taffy, Davidson, Revs and Hares.

Of the pilots, Lofty seemed the most infallible and Jimmy the most indestructible; Jimmy whose will-power was phenomenal and whose calm could not be shaken. He it was who had stayed in his plane though a fighter had put his starboard motor and his guns out of action. The enemy plane swooped round and round, closer and closer, playing cat and mouse.

Jimmy remained calm, and in the end the German fighter collided with the Whitley and crashed, whilst the Englishman, minus half a tail-plane, with one engine gone, staggering at only five hundred feet, crossed the Dutch coast and limped home to his base.

Desmond was to be his second pilot when he got his first command. He, too, was unflurried and made no mistakes. Yet before the year was out all of these fellow-flyers were dead, except Willy, who had become a prisoner-of-war. Cheshire had to learn the grim and tragic lesson that no amount of skill and experience alone can save a pilot over enemy soil. As well as those qualities he needs lots of luck.

In his first days on the squadron, however, nothing impinged on his mind except that he seemed totally unfamiliar with everything that was now supposed to be his workaday life. Everything was new, and everything had to be learnt— and there was much to learn. What speed to fly at, engine revolutions, boost, bomb-loads, guns, turrets, bomb-selector switches, bomb-sights, petrol cocks, engine pressures, crew drill, how to unhook a dinghy, navigation and wireless procedure, evasive action, ack-ack and searchlights.

"There were a maze of details running through my mind. Couldn't seem to sort them out. I'd figured you more or less got into your plane, took off, dropped your bombs, came back and that was that. I seemed to be learning!"

Nothing was as he had imagined it. Instead of just getting into your plane and taking off you had first to listen to the meteorological expert ("he had a large chart covered in curves and curious markings which I didn't understand at all"). Then came the Intelligence Officer, who talked briefly about the German advance. These were the days of Dunkirk. He pointed out the line the enemy had reached or rather, where Intelligence *thought* they had reached. Then came the Signals Officer with mysterious information about D.F. stations and identification procedure, and the C.O. with instructions about bombing heights, tactics and take-off times.

Not even then did one just take off and bomb the target. There were maps, rulers, compasses, dividers, a mechanical wind computer, pencils, rubbers, code-books, astro tables, a sextant, a planisphere, a protractor, a log book and Very cartridges to collect. There were boots, sid-cot, helmet, gloves, scarf, harness, parachute, oxygen tube and rations to be dispersed over one's body. There was the just-too-high hatch of his plane—Q for Queenie—to be crawled through ("very painful and most exhausting"). Only after this ritual could they take off and head for the target; in those days with Cheshire as an inexperienced second pilot and Lofty as his captain.

Even his first impression of enemy soil, German-occupied France, was not what he expected . . . "It looked just like England. Very surprising. One expects enemy-occupied soil to look different."

His first impression of ack-ack . . . "How slowly those tracers move. Peculiar. They go straight for a while and then start wavering about. They don't seem meant for us, so they can't be dangerous!"

His first impression of flares dropped to illumine the target . . . "They look just like fires on the ground and don't seem to light up anything. Only when they are very close to us can I tell whether they are a flare in the air or a fire on the ground. Then they blind me and I can't see anything anyway."

His first impression of his first mission . . . "I became utterly confused. Perhaps I spent too long staring at what was new to me."

Such were the early days. But he progressed quickly, always aiming at the cool, confident certainty of Lofty and Jimmy and the others. He discovered that dawn is not grey but mauve: that war is never what one expects . . . "not enough glamour and too much to learn": that flying is not romantic adventure but anything from six to fifteen hours of solid tedium. The monotony of flight only seemed to become something worth while if the enemy attacked with fighters and anti-aircraft fire and gave the mission some purpose.

It amused him to fly Whitley bombers over Germany because the noses of their two engines looked Jewish and purposeful and Jewish-looking engines over the Reich seemed ironic to Cheshire. He was fond of these motors with their snarling bellow: but he liked them best when, in the mauve dawn, their exhaust flames had changed from the fiery red of the darker hours to a pale, brassy flare. Then he knew he was safe and almost home.

He had often imagined himself, before he had ever actually flown on raids, being interviewed by Intelligence:

"Did you find the target?"

"Certainly."

"Did you hit it?"

"Of course."

He now knew that there was more to it than that. Bombing, he realized, was first and foremost a matter of technical skill and experience not of glamorous daring. Then, granted that skill and experience, it was a matter of complete crew co-operation and confidence (the confidence of the captain in himself, of the crew in themselves and of the crew in their captain) and flying ability.

He determined to learn to fly instinctively.

"I don't care how much I fly," he told his skipper Lofty, "I like it." So Lofty, who had long since tired of it, let him fly all he wanted. Lofty regarded his No. 2 as a little mad in this respect.

When Q for Queenie was not flying, Cheshire would blindfold himself and move round the plane until he could lay his hands on any piece of equipment without the use of eyesight. He mastered all the plane's mechanical intricacies, even its engines. For this he turned to the ground crew.

"Their anxiety to help me was the greatest stimulus I could ever want," he says.

That was the beginning of a very personal association with all his ground crews for Cheshire. All through his war career he maintained the closest contact with them. Always he was considerate of them and interested in them. Always he insisted upon their work being recognized as an integral part of the more spectacular tasks carried out by aircrews. As a result they worshipped him.

When he returned from a raid he resisted the temptation to sit back a second and relax in the cockpit, as one does in the driver's seat of a car after a long drive. Why? Because the ground crew were waiting to service the plane and it was late: one must not keep them up unnecessarily.

Winter 1940 came and, with it, heavy frosts. The crew closed all the blacked-out windows and sat huddled in flying suits, more for warmth than action, and filled the crew room with an almost impenetrable haze of cigarette smoke.

This is the picture that always returns strongest to Cheshire's mind when he recalls those days. The benches round the wall, men swaddled in flying kit and huddled together, men leaning over the tables with linoleum tops scarred by the black gash of cigarette burns, the harsh cut of a heel, the circular stains of cups and glasses.

Propaganda posters on the walls: and an illustration of how to launch an aircraft's rubber dinghy: talk of popsies swept off their feet by the irresistible ardour of the R.A.F.: talk of pubs and home: line-shooting and apprehension. When *would* the C.O. come and give them their orders?

They lit more cigarettes, shouted, slept, boasted and played childish practical jokes. Still the C.O. didn't come. Then the door opened—the door that never shut quite properly—and he was there. Now they would fly. How many of them, and who, would go missing tonight? The air was blue with smoke and the draught that came through that not-quite-shut door was icy.

In those days no one ever asked them what they were trying to accomplish, only *how* they were going to do it. They fought a war of counter-offensives, more often than not being shot-up by fighter intruders as they landed back home and straffed as they slept in their quarters. And always, night after night, for weeks and months (and, for Cheshire, for five years), they raided Europe. Time upon endless time the snouted Whitleys nosed their way over enemy soil; the harmless, impersonal-looking tracer drifted boozily up at him, and then they returned home.

It was over Duisberg that, for the first time, Cheshire heard one of those harmless, drifting tracers explode with a deep roar and felt it rock his aircraft viciously. He says of that time: "I had a sinking feeling. Somehow it was more than I had bargained for—and very, very personal." He sat on his parachute, hoping foolishly that it might protect him. Then, abruptly, the fear vanished. He was never afraid of ack-ack again. He remarked later: "Ack-ack changes these dull flights into something worth having. Something only war could give."

So, having learnt all this, he was given his captaincy. Desmond became his second pilot, Revs became his rear-gunner and Taffy became his navigator.

"Taffy had wavy fair hair, blue eyes and a scar below his chin. I liked him as soon as I saw him," Cheshire says. And certainly Taffy liked Cheshire.

For months the war then became his flights with his new

crew, particularly Desmond and Taffy. Desmond, who seemed unshakeable, and Taffy, who refused to worry about any flying hazards because he believed implicitly that the hazard had not yet been invented which his skipper could not overcome. Taffy who sang riotously, in the Welsh fashion, whenever he was pleased and was irrepressibly conversational over the intercom.

Cheshire, in his own book *Bomber Pilot*, recollects a typical crew conversation, garbled and incoherent with excitement, when on one occasion they had hit their target and the enemy had hit them.

·"Bombs gone."

"Bomb-sight too," announces Taffy, who has a shell splinter in the face.

"Bomb-sight too what?" demands Cheshire.

"Got it, got it: absolutely magnificent. Slap in the middle."

"Got *what?*" snarls Cheshire. "Desmond, go and see what's the matter with Taffy. He's probably bumped his head on the perspex."

"It's not Taffy, Captain," a voice announces, "it's me."

"Who the hell's me?"

"It's O.K., Cap., it's only a splinter. Carry on!"

"Thanks very much," responded a sarcastic skipper.

"Shall I open up?" another voice enquires.

"Open up what? Has everyone gone mad or is it me? Who are you?"

"Rear-gunner speaking."

"Bomb-sights disappeared, Captain."

"What the hell's the bomb-sight to do with the rear-gunner?"

"It's *not* the rear-gunner—it's Taffy."

"Well, I'll put you on a charge when we get back."

"*When!*" responds an unrepentant Welshman—and then the plane is hit again and the conversation stops. They return home and next day, all thought of "charges" forgotten, they drink beer together, all the crew, and await the adventures that the next night will bring.

Down at the pub they would drink pint after pint of beer, their arms round each other's shoulders, occasionally breaking loose to pursue some unsuspecting maiden who, in fact, suspected exactly the same as they did.

The piano would crash out "I'm gonna hang out the washing on the Siegfried Line" and "Run, Rabbit, Run" or "Roll out the Barrel." Intoxicated equally with alcohol and their own survival of yet another raid, they would sing uproariously and buy the pianist a drink. For the moment the next raid lay in the far, far future and only the moment mattered.

They were a good crew, Cheshire and Desmond, his wireless operator and Revs and Taffy. They were inseparable and happy together. The war was joyous and exhilarating in its camaraderie and excitement. And already they had the reputation of flying with a man who was lucky. Luck and determination, that was what you needed to survive a war in the air.

"The minute you see your target, go for it." That was Cheshire's philosophy. "Don't manœuvre for position. Too much time to lose your nerve. Just go for it. Get into trouble first and then worry about getting out afterwards."

His crew were happy with this decision. Happy because it worked, and because "Cheese," their skipper, was lucky; and because they were young men and those were the days of the war when young men were contented in their own company anyway.

Then came the time of Cologne and the flight that won a citation for both Cheshire and Davidson, his new wireless operator. Davidson was eighteen years old and this was his first mission.

They had been approaching their target steadily, through fierce ground fire, and something had gone wrong. Taffy's directions as navigator from the bomb-bay had ceased altogether. He seemed unable to locate their objective, although the night was still clear and visibility had never been better. His captain was anxious to bomb and get home. The ack-ack was ferocious. Somehow this night did not bode well.

After repeated enquiries for a course, to which Taffy made no answer, Cheshire snarled down the intercom: "Answer me, Taffy. Answer me, damn you."

But apparently the Welshman had lost all his confidence for he replied nothing. Meantime clouds began to roll in, threatening to obscure the target, and priceless minutes passed with no advice from the navigator.

"Look, Taffy," Cheshire cursed, ' if you can't pin-point yourself tonight, when it's as clear as this, you'd better give up navigation and take up tiddly-winks." No answer.

"Desmond, go and see what's the matter with him. Grab the maps. We'll do the navigation ourselves. Got that?"

"Yep," replied the imperturbable second pilot, and went off to rebuke Taffy.

Desmond returned after a short time. Deliberately he plugged in his intercom and settled himself into place. He was always deliberate. He always took his time. Cheshire fumed at the delay. As soon as he knew that Desmond could hear, he snapped:

"Well, what's the verdict?"

"Intercom must be U.S.—or else it's his helmet. He says he's been screaming instructions at you for the last twenty minutes. Knows exactly where we are but you won't lead him over the target."

Cheshire then learnt that they were twelve miles north of their target and that it was now too late to return because cloud had already covered it.

"Hell!" he cursed. "O.K., we'll go for Cologne instead. Go and tell Taffy. Tell him to aim for the marshalling yards.

He's to show which way I'm to turn by kicking his feet. You'll have to pass on which foot he's kicking. O.K.?"

"Yes, O.K."

"Oh Desmond ..."

"Yes?"

"Tell him I've been swearing at him but I didn't know what the trouble was and I'm sorry."

Then to Davidson, the wireless operator, whose job it was also to drop the flares: "About five minutes, Davey, and we'll want your flare. Sorry you've had so long on your ownsome ..." He remembered that it was Davidson's first flight and wondered how the lad was getting on. Mustn't let him feel too lonely.

So they headed for the Cologne marshalling yards, Taffy giving bearings by kicking his feet, Desmond passing those instructions on to Cheshire, Revs (the rear-gunner) peering round for night fighters, Davidson waiting over the bomb-bay with one flare ready to drop and another beside him to push out after the first.

They reached Cologne, a suspiciously quiet Cologne. No ack-ack: no searchlights: no fighters. Cheshire felt a heavy, irrational presentiment. It was a trap, he was sure of it. One lone British bomber over Cologne and every brain and faculty on the ground below watching and waiting for him, waiting till he reached just the right spot. He was sure of it.

Irritably Taffy was kicking his right foot.

"Right a little." The foot stopped still: both feet were still.

"Steady ..."

"LOOK OUT! TURN QUICK!! *OVER* ..."

Then came the explosion. A vicious flash and a roar in front of him, leaving him blind. Another crash and a horrifying glare of light from the rear. The plane bucketed and lurched and then careered groundwards. Cheshire's thoughts were chaotic.

"I'm blinded . . . no, it's only the flash . . . I feel sick . . . We'll have to bale out. Always wanted to try a jump. Not this way, though. Don't want to jump at all now. Anyway—where the hell is my 'chute? . . . No more letters from mother . . . What a foul smell. Can't breathe. Oxygen mask, that's the thing."

Frantically he tore off his gloves, found the press-stud of the mask and clipped it on. Glorious clean oxygen. Then, unconsciously, the training of a captain asserted itself.

"Have you dropped the bombs yet?" he demanded. The words surprised him. He hadn't thought them—they had just come. No answer. Yes, there was. A faint "I've been hit. I've been hit."

He remembered that awful flash behind him. They must all be dead or dying. The plane wallowed downwards; but he could see well enough now to check his altimeter. Five thousand feet it read. Strange—he thought they would have lost more height. He fought with sluggish controls and a reluctant machine. Gradually they levelled out—and the long Jewish snouts resumed their even roar of defiance. "Good old engines," he thought lovingly, "they never let you down."

A grotesque, blood-streaming figure appeared beside him. He could not recognize it and had no desire to look at it again to try and do so. The bloody apparition stood there a moment, apparently bemused. Then it looked back down the fuselage and screamed: "Fire. The tank's on fire."

"Well, put it out," snapped his voice. Again that subconscious ability to command. It astounded him and, doing so, brought him entirely to his senses. He was the captain of a wrecked, blazing bomber. He would fly it—nothing else mattered. And the bleeding figure, jolted by the peremptory orders of a seemingly unmoved skipper, promptly vanished to put out the fire near the petrol tank!

Cheshire wriggled in discomfort as his uniform stuck to

him moistly. His back was sweating with the heat of the flames to the rear. He looked behind him and saw thick, oily smoke and red gashes of fire. More shells from the ground, their explosions deafening now because the perspex hatch over his head was torn and the noise, like the wind, came roaring in. A rattle of splinters through the fuselage. Desmond appeared.

"Can you keep her in the air?" he asked.

"What do *you* think?"

That was all Desmond wanted to know. He returned and, with Taffy, deliberately crawled under the petrol tank and, fighting from the middle of the fire, put it out. They left their parachutes behind them to do so.

Half the plane's fuselage had vanished. The fire had been caused by a fragment of shell which exploded the first flare as "Davey" leant over it and just before it had dropped. Although in flames from head to foot himself, Davey had still thrown out the second flare so that it could not ignite and blow the bomber to bits.

Taffy came back to Cheshire, bleeding and glistening, but grinning broadly. They both roared with laughter. *And then they decided to drop their bombs as planned.*

"Davey" crawled up, his face a charred, crusted mask streaked with blood, his eyes two vivid, scarlet pools.

"I'm going blind, sir," he moaned. "I'm going blind." Cheshire was so appalled at the sight he could not look at it. He leant forward and concentrated on flying so that they could drop their bombs, Taffy once again lying in the bomb-bay and kicking his feet.

"Right, hard right," Desmond instructed.

"Go on—much further." So they turned and twisted in their drunken flight. "Steady" . . . Then the plane suddenly lifted gladly and Cheshire knew their bombs were away. "Wizard," announced Taffy gleefully. "Right in the middle of the yard." Now for home.

No maps! They had all either been blown out of the plane or burnt. And the mechanical wind computer was not working. Cheshire guessed a course of 310°. "Bound to hit something somewhere," he announced cheerfully, and so they set off for England.

Now that the action was over and their safe return depended mainly upon whether or not the shattered Whitley would hold together long enough, Cheshire had time to give thought to his crew.

"How's Davey?" he asked. Desmond told him. Though he was blind and in agony as well, Davidson was at his wireless set trying to get a course for the stricken plane.

"The Captain needs a fix," he kept repeating. He would tell Revs where to turn the dials so that his setting was correct and then have the rear-gunner guide his raw fingers on to the key. Message after message he tapped out. Fainting and moaning he kept trying. And it was only when they discovered that the wireless was U.S. anyway that they could persuade him to stop.

"Try and keep him out of the wind," Cheshire ordered, his vivid imagination telling him only too clearly how agonizing must be the icy air that poured through the torn fuselage and clawed at the blackened ribbons of the youngster's flesh.

"What's the temperature inside?"

"Sixteen below."

"Wrap him up as well as you can."

It was Revs who looked after him, nursing him in his arms all the way home. And it was Revs who, noticing that at least one of the parachutes had been destroyed by the fire, put his own on Davidson and then tied a piece of string to it so that if the Whitley, as seemed highly probable, began to disintegrate in mid-air they could fling the boy out and, by holding the end of the string, release his 'chute for him. That way he would have a chance; Revs, of course, would not.

So they flopped and lumbered on. Back across Europe in the dawn and early morning light they flew. A flashing light appeared on the English coast at ten to seven: Cromer and a perfect landfall. The first time they had ever achieved a perfect landfall, and it had to be this time with no maps, wireless or instruments. The gods were with them. At five to eight they landed in front of the control tower and Davey was rushed to hospital. He had returned from his first operational flight.

"These eighteen-year-olds," commented Cheshire, with the awful knowledge of one who has himself reached the age of twenty-three, "are a remarkable breed of men."

Later the citation arrived and Cheshire attended the first of his four investitures. He was awarded the D.S.O.

"*Showing great coolness,*" the citation read, "*Pilot Officer Cheshire regained control of his aircraft, which had lost considerable height and was being subjected to intense anti-aircraft fire, and although the explosion had blown out a large part of the fuselage and caused other damage he managed to regain height ... Although the aircraft was only partially answering the controls Pilot Officer Cheshire succeeded in returning to his aerodrome.*"

Davidson, after a series of operations, regained his sight, recovered from his burns and lived to fight another day. He was decorated with a D.F.M.

But for Desmond and Taffy who had saved the plane, recklessly disregarding their own safety by fighting and extinguishing a fire that raged near a petrol tank, and for Revs who sacrificed his own parachute to Davey, there was nothing.

It is not possible to award all the members of every plane that returns thus bravely home.

"But it knocked everything a bit flat for me," says Cheshire. That is his attitude towards all his decorations: everyone else deserved them equally or more.

Chapter Five

THE WAR HARDENS

FROM THIS TIME onwards the war was never again to hold the ferociously exciting zest of its earlier months for Cheshire. Battling his way home in a plane that squashed along, torn almost in halves, with one of his crew frightfully burnt and maimed, he suddenly became aware of the conflict as something which offered death and carnage to youth rather than excitement. Henceforth he flew with the relentless determination of a man bent on destroying the enemy, but no longer so gaily or with such relish.

In no small degree this was due to the splitting up of his crew. Desmond got his own plane to command and Taffy was posted away from the squadron: Desmond who had so perfectly balanced his skipper's buoyant high-spirits with his own equable good humour: Taffy whose infectious Celtic enthusiasm had never failed to cheer.

Gloomily Cheshire reflected on the loss of the fair-haired Welshman: on how he had always worked away at his maps and bombing and then, his job done, regardless of the perils surrounding them, invariably gone to sleep! How he had roared with enthusiasm over the intercom and sung riotously whenever they hit their target, and no threats of disciplinary action could stop him. How he had laughed when things were bad and abused the enemy ground defences for their inaccuracy ... "You think we're over there, you bastards, don't you?"

he had mocked. "Well, we're bloody well not ... We're here!" Yes, Taffy had been a tower of strength.

Desmond approached him, dressed to take off.

"Know where Taffy is?" he asked.

"No," said Cheshire, "getting ready to move, I suppose. Do you want him specially?"

Desmond explained he wanted to say good-bye and give him some cigarettes, fifty Players, his mother had sent for each of the old crew.

"I'll see if I can find him," Cheshire offered.

Desmond thanked him, and asked him, too, to have a look for his wireless operator's mascot which was also missing. Neither Taffy nor the mascot could be found: so, leaving messages and cigarettes to be delivered by Cheshire to the Welshman, Desmond took off.

He took off into a fiery dawn and, before the early flames had flickered out of the sky, he collided over the North Sea with an incoming German bomber ... and died.

Three weeks later Lofty, Cheshire's first captain in Q for Queenie, was shot down and also died. Lofty, who had taught him so much, who had seemed so utterly steadfast and certain of himself—gone now, as so many others were going. The war was hardening.

So the first winter ended, cold and comfortless in every way, the only bright spot being the near presence, also in a Whitley squadron, of his young brother Christopher.

When he heard that he was being posted away from 102 Squadron to No. 35 Halifax Squadron, he did not really mind. With Lofty and Desmond and Taffy gone, the old Whitley days no longer seemed the same.

As soon as he had transferred to Halifaxes he again set about his relentless self-imposed task of getting to know intimately every inch of the new aircraft. Once more, on non-flying days, he roamed round inside the plane, blindfold and groping, until he had the safe, sure touch of the sensitive sightless in their own well-known home.

Once again he talked with and questioned the ground crew about maintenance and motors, four motors now, not two. That was even better than Whitleys. And once again, by mixing with them so easily and asking questions so frankly, he won the confidence and affection of the men who serviced his plane. Cheshire has always liked to be liked. Contrary, though, to the experience of many who share this desire (a desire which can also be a weakness) he has the capacity to ensure that he is.

So, steadily, he grew more familiar with the new aircraft— more familiar than most, because Halifaxes were just off the production line and none had had any experience of them, and not many were as assiduous in their desire to learn as he was. The weeks passed into months: the training of practice flights only continued. Fully occupied with work, he missed just one thing, the tight-knit bond of crew camaraderie.

And then came what seemed a miracle. Taffy walked into the crew room.

"I've come to join you, sir," said the Welshman.

"Good old Taffy," shouted Cheshire, and they fell into each others' arms.

"Wizard, Cheese," enthused Taffy, and all the other sergeants watched this shocking display of disrespect for an officer's rank with obvious astonishment.

Now, more happily, training continued. And, to add to their contentment, Revs turned up. He had survived a crash in the North Sea and, because of his work in rescuing others of the crew on that occasion, he had been given the choice of where he would go.

"To Mr. Cheshire," he asked. And so, to Mr. Cheshire, he went.

Then came their first operational flight in a Halifax,

against Kiel. To their regret, Revs had not been allowed to accompany them: but at least they carried the mascot he had designed specially for them, a cat holding Hitler's head between its paws. A lucky cat because Cheshire was lucky. Rev's place at the tail-gun was taken by a small, cheerful youngster, with a mind of his own, called Hares.

The ack-ack was not only intense over Kiel, it was also accurate. It displeased Taffy enormously because it holed their plane repeatedly, and this the Welshman regarded as untidy. However, his good humour was soon restored when a German fighter attacked and Hares, with the enemy's opening burst, volunteered his first speech of the night!

"Come in, you bastard," he roared, "Come in, you lousy, flat-faced bastard! Come on. I'll give you what you're waiting for! *I'll teach you to come messing round with our Mr. C!*" As these words crackled over the intercom all Taffy's displeasures vanished and he bounced up and down in his seat with joy, shouting with laughter and himself exclaiming "Wizard," and "Cheese."

But the past three months of comparative inactivity, the lack of hostile activity, that is, had chafed on Cheshire. Thirty thousand Axis prisoners had been captured by the Army at Bardia in January 1941: the Lotofen Isles had been raided by a special pre-Commando force in March: there had been a revolution in Yugoslavia and King Peter has assumed control: the Navy had won a superb victory at Matapan: the Germans had invaded Greece and Albania in April: the Australians had withdrawn to Tobruk and there stubbornly refused to surrender: Athens fell and the remnants of the R.A.F. in Greece were evacuated to Crete. All this whilst he flew on only one sortie against the enemy.

All this, and the closing stages of the Battle of Britain, a battle in which some fifty-two squadrons of assorted British fighter aircraft resisted the onslaught of 2,000 front-line

German planes, whose object was to destroy London and keep the likes of Cheshire permanently on the ground. The radar invented by Watson Watt, the tireless devotion of ground crews, who kept every plane capable of becoming airborne in the sky, and the matchless skill and daring of the fighter pilots themselves all united to foil the Luftwaffe. Yet Cheshire himself felt frustrated and useless at this stage of the war.

In short, apart from training flights and the one raid with Taffy and Hares, he had done little since his transfer that he could call exciting.

Nor, it seemed, was he destined to. Halifaxes being very much in their infancy, it was suddenly decided to ground the whole squadron whilst various modifications were carried out. In the meantime, it was decreed, two of the pilots were to proceed to the United States to assume special duties over there. These two were to be chosen by lot and the privilege fell to Cheshire and a New Zealander called Willy.

Both men were rather pleased at the prospect of a trans-atlantic interlude. They packed and prepared for the voyage with enthusiasm. Typically, just before he left the squadron, Cheshire visited the C.O. and requested that his crew, none of whom had had the long break from actual hostilities that he himself had enjoyed in the past training period, should be rested until his return. This, in so far as it was possible in war-time, the C.O. promised. Whereupon, quite happily, Cheshire set off with Willy to join the huge liner that would take them comfortably across to America.

The huge liner turned out to be a 900-ton Norwegian vessel which was conspicuous for its lack of comfort. When they realized that this was slightly smaller than a Channel packet steamer they quickly decided that the trip was no privilege at all but a calculated insult and a great mistake.

"What's more," Cheshire complains, "they used words

like *abaft* and *aloft* and *scuppers* and *galley* quite shamelessly, without at any time making any attempt to explain what they meant. To make matters worse I was tricked into playing cards all day; then, when the voyage ended, when I was owed over £20, they said that that was far too much and gave me £3 10s. instead."

Altogether Cheshire did not greatly enjoy surface travel in convoy. Sinkings were too frequent and when they received news that the *Bismarck*, having just sunk the *Hood*, was heading for them as its next prey, the flyer became really unhappy. Became unhappy not because of the added danger but because the language of the naval types at once grew more technical than ever, to the point of being incomprehensible, and nothing annoys Cheshire more than something he cannot understand.

But they survived their Atlantic crossing, the *Bismarck* notwithstanding, and he and Willy reported, as instructed, to Canadian Pacific. There, it seemed, no one had ever heard of them nor of the fact that they were to fly a plane back across the Atlantic to Britain. So, leaving a forwarding address, they departed promptly for New York to enjoy themselves whilst the authorities made up their minds.

America, at this time, was still not at war. After two years of combat, rationing, restrictions and daily danger in Britain, Cheshire and Willy now found themselves in a city which knew nothing of bombing and shortages, which regarded danger as something romantic and strange, which disported itself with all the brisk confidence and gaiety of a country whose life is not only normal and peaceful but also prosperous.

To the British airmen this atmosphere of carefree security was intoxicating. And, of all the people they met, none was more carefree and delightful than an actress called Constance Binney. She had the sophistication of a wealthy woman whose friends were celebrities: her wardrobe was expensive and attractive to the male eye: her sense of humour bubbled with the champagne zest of high-living uninhibited by war. She was everything which the European conflict had denied to young Cheshire. He represented the youth of Europe upon whom death was taking so unnatural a toll: she represented Femininity and Peace and unanxious, joyous living.

Constance made the two British airmen feel thoroughly at home. A Union Jack was draped over the porch and Constance's mother raised her glass and announced: "To the devil with that fiend and God bless England for boys like you two." Aggressively Willy spoke up. "What about New Zealand?" he demanded, but the intricacies of our Imperial affiliations were too much for the American mentality which saw the whole Commonwealth as "England," so he won no concessions for the Dominions after all.

Conversation among them was epigrammatic and witty. They all had a flair for words. To quote again from *Bomber Pilot*, "A woman is as old as she looks and a man is old when he stops looking," declared Miss Binney, whose age was separated from that of her guests by more than a generation. They battled with wisecracks and rocked with laughter.

Their daily life became studded with the names and company of celebrities.

"George composed some of the 'Rhapsody in Blue' on this," said Constance, pointing at her piano.

"George?"

"Gershwin," she told him casually. "Used to come back here and strum on it every night after the show. Mother got furious and kicked him out every night at five to two. If it hadn't been for her I should have married him."

And so it went on. They became drugged, all three of them, by the excitement of the new lives they offered one another. To the actress—British humour and understatement, youth and heroism and the romance of war. To the flyers—American exuberance, endless parties, the brittle wit of stage people and the romance of peace. Cheshire in particular, sensitive and with a humour superbly attuned to a joy in the ridiculous, revelled in it.

Little wonder, then, that in a matter of weeks, during which time she had been his constant companion and hostess, he and Constance Binney married. They married in spite of his better judgement, which told him that the environment in which he found himself was an unnatural one: in spite of his recognition that she was much his senior and that such a disparity in age must inevitably over-tax the strength of a bond with a very young man: particularly, or perhaps because of it, they married in spite of the advice of all their friends.

But, for a while at least, the marriage brought Cheshire contentment and peace of mind. It has never, even though now dissolved, brought him any sadness. Three days after the wedding he flew home to Britain in a Hudson, a proud and happy husband.

His happiness, however, was short-lived. When he returned to his squadron mess he was greeted by Revs.

"What sort of a trip did you have?"

"Fine," Cheshire told him. "Bit monotonous, except for the icebergs and the Northern Lights." The words reminded him of his plan as an undergraduate to fly the Atlantic in an old biplane, with the college boiler-man as his navigator, and he smiled. But Revs was talking again.

"Did you bring a Liberator?"

"No. They wouldn't trust me with one. Packed me off in a Hudson."

"Tell me about your wife." Cheshire advised Revs to wait till he met her: and then thanked him for being a reception committee.

"I wish there were more to meet you," the gunner replied. And, to Cheshire's quick-flung question as to who was missing, he answered: "All the crew. Every single one except me."

Cheshire felt himself shrinking from news that was doubly appalling because he had been certain that the crew would not have to fly whilst he was away. The C.O. had promised it, if it were possible.

Hares had been killed when his plane crashed vertically into the ground, followed by a Me.110. He had maintained his fire from the tail-gun right up to the last moment. Cheshire nodded. One would expect that of Hares.

The second pilot had died in a Fortress.

Taffy had been shot down over Germany. The last thing he said before taking off was: "When is Mr. C. coming back?"

Saddened, Cheshire went off for a drink. Next day they gave him a new crew and the war continued. Berlin, Cologne, Duisberg, Berlin, Essen and again Berlin. It became routine, but it was different now from what it had been.

Different because of the German ground defences, where now there were four or even ten guns to every one that had fired at them before: different because where there had previously been fifty or sixty searchlights which were effective only up to 8,000 feet, now there were two or three hundred, effective up to 18,000 feet. Different because of the barrage of shells that greeted them all the way from Denmark to Berlin; because of the more numerous night-fighters: because of the host of knobs and technical instruments with which they had to contend in the bombers of 1941, aids they would have scorned in 1940 and found aggravating in the extreme now. Different because the first fierce, joyous elation of the war had gone: because the first comrades of the war had gone: because promotion and added responsibilities had arrived.

Chapter Six

DEAD OR MISSING

THERE ARE MANY blanks as to the past in the memory of the Cheshire of today, especially where those periods were particularly unproductive or now seem distasteful. One could almost suspect a psychological flight, a *fugue*, from these moments of other years—a refuge in forgetfulness. And, if this be so, why not?

It could well be that after fifty or so flights with a crew with whom he identified himself entirely his memory now revolts against recalling in too-clear detail the flights that followed the loss of all those earlier comrades. The degree of his reluctance to recollect can be gathered from the questions and answers that follow, a reluctance that diminishes as his mind gets away from personalities and on to action.

"Have you got any impressions of that time at all?"

"Not many."

"Well, how about decorations?"

"Nothing much. D.F.C. at the end of my first tour."

"What for?"

"Can't remember."

"How many trips did you do on that first tour?"

"About fifty—actually it was two tours run into one." And here the frozen memory thawed with the warmth of the recollection of having squeezed two tours into one, of having escaped a desk and an instructor's job. He smiled happily, a wide, infectious grin; and then, without a qualm, spoke about the war that had followed.

He has only two vivid recollections of this second tour. The first concerns an emergency landing in Britain after a trip to Berlin. Most of the way home his engineer had assured him they were running out of petrol.

"Nonsense," said Cheshire, who could see no sense in agreeing, even if the man were right. Then, without warning, one of the Halifax's engines cut. Soon a second cut—both outer motors were dead. They saw a field ahead, flashed emergency and, in the face of a torrent of red-flashed refusals from the control tower which he disregarded completely, except that they nearly blinded him, Cheshire landed at the same time as a Whitley, neither knowing nor caring whether they were into wind or not.

When they rolled to a standstill there was a second's silence. Then the engineer spoke: "I told you so," he said.

At this time there came a genuinely bright ray of sunshine. News, and good news. Taffy and the others of his crew who flew with him on that last flight before Cheshire's return were all safe. Prisoners-of-war, but safe. It pleased Cheshire to think that the Welshman's irrepressible good spirits and capacity for song had not, after all, been silenced for ever.

On another trip, over Berlin, Cheshire states calmly: "I remember deliberately disobeying orders as to the route. I felt sure the planned route would be disastrous. *So we took another.*" This is his second clear memory of that period and he broke into a delightful smile in recollection of it, warmed with a mixture of war-time nostalgia and the joy of cocking a snook at authority. "Just as well we did," he continued. "*We* got there free of ack-ack: but over on our port side going, and on our starboard coming back" (the planned route), "the barrage never ceased."

Probably he remembers that night and his unauthorized route so clearly because it was from this raid that his brother failed to return, Christopher the family favourite, now missing, perhaps killed, somewhere over Berlin.

There had been many personal losses to Cheshire in the war so far but none to compare with this. Odd snatches of a past conversation came back to him.

"Keep it going, Chesh. This is the fourth time you've been over the target together. You've created a record already." That had been the Intelligence Officer speaking.

And they had kept it going. A raid on the hydrogen works at Gelsenkirchen had resulted in four direct hits. Sheets of vast, blue-green flame. Christopher had been there too. And then Berlin, only this time Christopher had not returned. To all his enquiries the answer was always the same: "No news." But the war had to go on.

Again over Germany ("I've forgotten where," Cheshire states). Heavy ack-ack. "Try cutting your motors," someone had advised. "Tricks the ground detectors." They were trapped by exploding shells so Cheshire tried it. They glided soundlessly and wheeled around on their tracks, the shells continuing to explode where their plane had last been heard. It worked. But the motors, when at first they tried to restart them, didn't! And when eventually they did, they both started on the one side and the plane wallowed. Then an explosion lifted them into a steep bank from which Cheshire seemed unable to extricate himself. The Halifax went more and more over on her side and lost height in a rapid spiral.

"Stand by to bail out," he commanded. The rear-gunner ran up to the hatch to obey, much to the amazement of the mid-gunner, who hadn't been listening and suddenly saw one of the crew about to fling himself into space. Deciding that the rear-gunner had gone mad, the mid-gunner fought strenuously to detain him.

"Dreadful scene," comments Cheshire laconically. "Anyway, Jock, the navigator, didn't move at all. He just kept

saying '*Come on, Chesh, you can do better than that*,' until I
snapped out of it. I realized then that, just when we'd been
thrown over on our side by ack-ack, the other two motors,
the port engines, had started again at full throttle and were
driving us round and round and further and further over. I
throttled back, she levelled out, and we stooged off home."

A few weeks passed. His colleague Jimmy, whom he had
regarded as imperishable, just as he had regarded Lofty as
infallible, was shot down and killed.

"Anything can happen to anyone if Jimmy goes," Willy
remarked soberly. And almost immediately he, too, went
missing. His closest friends and associates from the first days
of combat had been these two, Lofty, Lousy, Frammy,
Desmond, Taffy and Revs. Now only Revs remained. No one,
it seemed, could escape for ever.

Maybe they could not escape completely but news arrived
within the next few days which indicated that they need not
vanish into oblivion. Christopher and Willy were both alive
and well, as prisoners-of-war.

Christopher's plane had suffered a hit on the tail-plane,
which made the aircraft uncontrollable and killed the rear-
gunner. The machine dived steeply. Christopher gave the
order to jump. Wireless operator, observer and second pilot
left the plane—only the engineer and Christopher remained,
Christopher nearest the hatch and every second vitally
important. He stepped aside, over the hatch, and insisted that
his engineer jump first.

"What a difference it makes to life," wrote Cheshire, "to
have a brother to be proud of."

Willy's news was less explicit. He was alive and well. He
was in the same camp as Christopher. His main worry was a
favourite cap he had left lying round somewhere. Would
Cheshire please find it and look after it?

Then came Cheshire's third war-time birthday, and soon

after it a flight over Berlin with Revs. When they returned to their base he was told that he was being grounded. His tour was over.

"Any decorations?" he was asked by a journalist.

"No, none," he smiled. "Very dull tour."

"What happened to Revs?"

"He was killed later—training to be a pilot." And so went the last of his first companions.

Chapter Seven

THE LUCKY SURVIVE

THERE COMES A TIME, to all men who fight wars, which is known to bull-fighters as "the moment of truth." This period of quiet between tours was to be Cheshire's moment of truth. He faced up boldly to the fact that wars were not, as he had thought in 1938, the heaven-sent fulfilment of youth's natural desire for excitement and action, rather that they were something entirely contrary to the spirit of youth, something implicitly destructive of it.

Talking to him today, one is conscious of what would appear to be a deliberately postponed youth. This is something one finds in many men who have survived an active and distinguished war career. It is almost as if, during the conflict, they had appreciated that the hot-headed rashness of immaturity itself could kill them just as surely as enemy fire. It is also as if they had appreciated that there could be no madder way of spending those precious and irreplaceable years than in the business of killing. Therefore, coldly and deliberately, they put their youth aside and became men. When the war was over, then they would return to the years they had deferred.

In the meantime, between the actual moments of conflict, these prematurely old men assume an artificial façade of immature "joie de vivre." Childishly they get drunk, make love and have fights, gamble and swear. Carefully they nourish their hothouse bloom of high-living and irresponsibility. Then, when the war stops, they return to take up again the threads of normal life, those threads that were broken at the age of nineteen or twenty. And though they be twenty-six or twenty-seven when they do so, though they have, in many respects, the wisdom of men three times their age, they eagerly clutch the carefully-hoarded-away years and draw on them slowly and with the sane economy their maturity has taught them.

This may not be so but certainly, in Cheshire, it seems the only explanation of that boyish sense of gaiety and fun, at the age of thirty-seven or so, that bubbles up in him so lightly today. And it seems, too, the only explanation of the boisterous and adolescent exuberance of all servicemen at war, most especially the R.A.F.

Whether this is the case or not, the fact remains that, by the time he had reached the age of twenty-three, Cheshire had become a wholly efficient machine of war and had achieved notoriety as one possessed of a driving determination, stripped of any mere youthful spirit of adventure, and aiming solely at forcing home his attacks against the enemy and destroying them.

He had also come to know himself as a flyer very well. He had a D.S.O. and a D.F.C. and no illusions at all about his skill or genius with aircraft.

"I was never what you would call a good pilot," he declares now with deadly seriousness. "But I did have a certain *flair* and I *was* lucky. Everyone knew I was lucky." He paused for a moment, probably thinking back over moments where luck had saved him, not skill. Where skill could not have saved him.

"Actually," he continued, "I was a rather indifferent pilot. My cockpit drill was terrible. That is, when I did it: often I just forgot it. Always hated it. And if I left off flying for more than a day then I flew shockingly. Conscious flying, no˙ instinctive. I got into the habit of flying every day to overcome

this. If we weren't bombing I used to go out on a practice run."
He paused again.

"You see it's bad to be preoccupied with the technique of flying. You should do it quite instinctively. Then, if anything crops up, you've got your whole mind free to cope with it. I'll give you an example.

"It was at Woodhall Spa one night. We were returning from a raid and when we got to the aerodrome there was an enemy plane in the area. This Jerry fighter was shooting up our aircraft as they landed.

"So as not to help him at all there were no signals from the field, just the landing flares along the strip. And all of us were circling round and round, waiting for our turn to land.

"Anyway, I hadn't flown for four days and all the time I was thinking about flying, about how steeply to bank. Always hated banking at night. Only used to do very gentle ones.

"On one of these turns, over my shoulder I spotted the light of the bomber behind me. Well, with all this banking and conscious flying I got the various lights mixed up—the ones on the landing field and the ones I could see over my shoulder. Next thing I know, instead of being well up in the air, I'm heading straight for a tree. Very nearly hit it. Now if I *had* hit it everyone would have said: 'Cheshire would never fly straight into the ground. Cheshire would never hit a tree. There must have been something wrong with the plane!' But there wasn't. It was just that I was a pretty inefficient devil and that I always needed practice." This then was Cheshire's moment of truth, and it was about his flying. He was to experience another later, about his courage. For the present, though, he had learnt enough.

"I didn't really have a talent for flying," he repeats, "just a flair and luck."

In October 1941 his wife arrived in England and they were photographed together by the Press. Asked how she managed to achieve her ambition to join her husband (she was the first bride of a British serviceman to cross the Atlantic in a troopship) she replied: "I have no idea. I just said to an official: *'I have married an Englishman called Cheshire and I want to go and join him!'* I believe my husband made some arrangements in England too—anyway, here I am." It seems that Constance shared her husband's capacity for understatement and humour.

Together they visited the family home. The American actress, mature and super-sophisticated, seemed strangely out of place in the supremely British and studious atmosphere of the Cheshire home. Later Cheshire took his wife to Oxford to see his old college. They met Bert, whom Constance found "cute." The scout was so astounded by the change wrought upon this most high-spirited of all his young gentlemen. "Very quiet and serious he was—not at all like he used to be". At his old school, as everywhere, his wife was accepted with a quiet British reserve that contrasted strangely with the open-hearted hospitality Cheshire had himself received when he had been in the United States.

Such failure of his marriage to impress either his family, especially in the absence of Christopher, or his compatriots cannot help having accelerated the change in Cheshire's character at this time. It was a change from boyish and somewhat shy geniality into wholly adult self-possession, the assurance of a man who conceives many original ideas of his own and sticks to them relentlessly until either they are accepted by others or replaced in his own mind by something better.

So far the war had taught him only to fight furiously, to destroy and to survive. He appreciated that luck played equally as strong a rôle in that survival as skill. He confessed that, though an ace pilot should know where every enemy shell will burst, all things being equal, only the lucky pilot, ace or otherwise, since all things never are equal, can evade the shell that explodes neither where he anticipated its explosion nor where the enemy gun-crew intended it. The weather affects the fuse or charge of a shell; a conscript Czech in the Skoda works deliberately makes an inefficient projectile; a gunner lays inaccurately, then the shell explodes where no one can have known it would explode. Only luck can guide one out of the path of such unintentioned blasts. Cheshire knew it and gave thanks that he was lucky.

So, exploiting his luck and holding steadfastly to his policy of not worrying about danger, just getting into it as quickly as possible, because then one had every incentive to get out of it again, he had fought his courageous and conventional war.

But now, flung back within himself a little by the loss of his friends and the failure of his marriage to achieve marked popularity at home in Britain, he turned his attention not merely to the waging of war but to the improving of the means of waging it, to the asserting of his own personality as a pilot and to the perfecting of the Cheshire technique of leading.

With a promotion in rank to that of Wing Commander, he now took himself and his slightly changed conception of things to 76 Squadron. It was September 1942.

Chapter Eight

THE NEW WAR

FOR their deeper thrusts into enemy territory, 76 Squadron of Halifaxes had achieved a reputation because the new four-engined bombers had a longer range than their two-motored sisters, the Whitleys. Essen, Emden, Kiel, Hanover, Mannheim and Berlin all suffered under the squadron's hammer blows. Now even Italy itself, so securely and smugly in the war as France fell, was not any longer to escape retribution from the air.

The year had been one of vast Axis activity nevertheless. Malta was bombed continuously; Malaya and Singapore, Indonesia and the Philippines, the western half of Russia, Tobruk and northern Africa almost up to Alexandria itself had all fallen into the enemy maw. But on October 23rd, the Battle of El Alamein, and on November 2nd, the Battle of Stalingrad, were the signals of a new war for the Allies—a war on the offensive.

By November 22nd the Russians had turned the tide completely in their sphere, whilst the Axis troops in Africa were in full retreat. By December 30th the Japanese troops in New Guinea were split in two by an Allied wedge driven straight through the jungle to the sea. All over the world the Axis drive had come to a grinding, mortal halt.

Thus, shortly after his arrival at 76 Squadron, a changed Cheshire took part in a changed war. He was a man suddenly inspired with new ideas which he was prepared aggressively to put forward. The war now became a conflict freshly inspired by the strange taste of victory which was hungrily sought after and savoured with relish by young men who had so long been on the defensive.

Thus as the battle of El Alamein was reaching its climax Cheshire's bombers pounded Genoa. The day after Montgomery recaptured Tobruk and announced: "We have completely smashed the German and Italian Armies," the same city was again bombed. As the Russians launched their counter-offensive at Stalingrad, the R.A.F. dropped 8,000-pounders on Turin. When Goebbels and Goering addressed the German people and armies in Berlin on the occasion of the tenth anniversary of Hitler's regime, Mosquitos bombed the Nazi capital. In February, 146,000 German dead were counted at Stalingrad and the remainder of the enemy force of 300,000 surrendered. Bomber Command, and 76 Squadron as part of it, were out every day and on twenty-four of the twenty-eight nights of that month.

This, then, is the background of Cheshire's next tour. And yet, again, when asked about this period, he merely purses his lips against joined finger-tips, looks rather vague—and not much interested—and announces:

"76 Squadron. Yes. Well, they made me a Wing Commander. Can't remember much else except it was 1942. Oh, and I distinctly remember the occasion when we were flying home from Genoa. Never forget it!"

They had just successfully bombed the Italian city. To do so, they had flown a long and arduous course over the Alps. Now they had to do it again, in reverse, to get home. They were tired and jaded with the nervous exhaustion that arrives when a dangerous job is done but hours of tedious flying lie ahead. Cheshire was flying on *George*, his automatic pilot, and had gone to sleep.

He was woken by fierce gun-fire and found an enemy biplane fifty yards away on their tail, firing point-blank.

"He missed. My rear-gunner never fired on him at all. I took violent evasive action but he got within fifty yards again. And again he missed.

"I was a bit petrified for a while. Fortunately, after that, the other plane couldn't hope to catch us again so we stooged off home. Just about the closest I ever got to being shot down by a fighter all the same. He just *couldn't* have missed, but he did. Twice! So I remember it rather well."

As a Wing Commander, Cheshire was only supposed to fly once a month unless exceptional circumstances arose. He did not have a crew of his own. It is extraordinary how many "exceptional circumstances," in the six months that followed, Cheshire was able to contrive. He usually managed two trips a month, and once achieved three.

He has joyous memories still of the trip he did when he returned so low through Rotterdam that small arms bullets fired from roof-top level were found to have lodged in his wings *from above*. This had been a 1,000 bomber raid on Cologne.

When asked why he returned so low, thundering through Rotterdam at street-level, he smiled.

"Well, the Briefing Officer said we had to. Whether we liked it or not." And then, grinning more mischievously than ever, he added: "And, besides, the Briefing Officer was in *my* plane!"

It was here, too, in 76 Squadron, as a Wing Commander, that Cheshire first fully revealed his genius for getting people to do things for him. Not only to do them, but to want to do them.

Ground crew, who had always been so devoted to him, he now organized into a club. This meant that all ground crews met once a month, under the title of "The Plumbers' Club," and discussed every conceivable aspect of their various trades. They had an emblem for their club, which was a large monkey-wrench held in an oily fist, and beneath it was printed the exhortation to their aircrew colleagues, "You bend 'em: we mend 'em."

As a result of this morale-building institution, where all grievances could be aired, all information pooled and flyers could meet technicians, 76 Squadron, in spite of almost continuous activity against the enemy, led the whole of Bomber Command in the number of planes always available for service.

Nor was this the only respect in which Cheshire's leadership by example secured results. On one day of citations alone, six of his flyers were decorated: and in one of his crews alone, of its seven members, five had won awards. None of this, he maintains now, can he particularly recollect.

Even the efficiency of the troublesome Halifaxes in those days was in no small way due to the unorthodox genius of 76 Squadron's Wing Commander.

Losses of Halifaxes at that time were particularly and inexplicably heavy. They were inclined, fully loaded and at maximum height, suddenly to fall into a fatal downwards spiral, their rudders locked over, and crash.

"Too heavy. Too much equipment," maintained Cheshire. He demanded to be allowed to remove kidney-cowls over the exhausts (let enemy fighters see the exhaust flames), part of the front turret, the mid-upper turret and much of the armour-plate.

He was furiously opposed by all except his A.O.C., Air Vice-Marshal Carr. But eventually the offending equipment was removed, and losses promptly fell. Again, as with so many events that are flattering to him, though he will always remember someone saying he had been afraid, he does not recall this success.

But he does have painful recollections of a celebration in York with Willie Tait. Never averse to a party of any kind, Cheshire accompanied his fellow pilot on this occasion. On the way home the car somehow turned itself over, the celebration apparently having been better than either pilot suspected, and Cheshire was hurled out, head foremost, straight through the roof.

"I was a bit concussed," he admits casually, rubbing his head reflectively. "They put me in 'dock' because of it: but I wasn't happy there, so I talked my way out of it in a couple of days and went back to the squadron."

For the next three months, however, he was to pay the price for this excess of zeal. He tired over-quickly and he found himself exhausted on each flight, not by the time he returned, but by the time he had reached his target.

The return trips became a nightmare of throbbing brain and wandering attention. Each time he forced himself to take off again, hoping things would have improved. And always the trouble was just as bad as, or worse than, it had been before.

"Had a bit of a bad time of it those months," he admits laconically.

But certainly he made no mention of this "bad time" and allowed no evidence of his growing weariness to creep into the many Press interviews that now inevitably came his way. Consider the marked understatement in this quote by Cheshire to *The Times* in January 1943 concerning a raid on Berlin:

"Batteries of guns and searchlights that once made Berlin the hottest place in all Germany for R.A.F. raiders have been moved to meet German needs on other fronts from Russia to the French Atlantic Coast.

"That is why the flak was so light, and only one plane was lost when a great force of four-engined Lancasters, Halifaxes and Stirlings unloosed a huge weight of bombs—including many four-tonners—on Saturday night."

Yet this attack, lasting about one hour, had been the biggest so far of the war. It was one of the most dazzlingly successful efforts of the R.A.F. since 1939.

Aircrews on their return had stated that the Berlin defenders made the poorest defence of any key town in Germany since heavy raids had begun eighteen months before.

Cheshire, who had at that time already made seven raids on Berlin, continued tersely: "It used to be the hottest place in Germany, with hundreds of guns and searchlights; but, instead of a wall of anti-aircraft fire, the flak tonight was negligible compared with my previous experiences over there. For example, I saw only one searchlight."

One Lancaster had circled round for forty minutes, the flak was so light. It had made three runs over the target. On the third run the bomb-aimer got his 8,000-pound bomb down.

This was the raid in which the R.A.F. avenged the Luft-waffe's heaviest raid on Britain when slightly less than 450 tons of bombs were dropped on London on the night of April 16th–17th, 1941. On this night men could see Berlin's fires a hundred miles away in the returning bombers. Yet Cheshire merely stated that the defences were light and that a lot of bombs, some of them four-tonners, had been dropped.

Thus, for the first time, Berliners experienced the indescribable devastation caused by 8,000-pound bombs, which were twice the size of those that Bomber Command had dropped on the city in its first raids fourteen months earlier.

One wonders what agonies of strain and exhaustion 76 Squadron's C.O. went through on the flight home from Berlin that night when he reported that the ack-ack was light but not that he was having a bit of a bad time.

During that "bit of a bad time," there was also an exchange of letters between Ace Pilot Captain Grigori Katseba, on behalf of the Russian Air Force, and Ace Pilot Cheshire himself, on behalf of the R.A.F.

"*How can I find words to express my admiration for your*

brilliant raids on Cologne, Essen and other German cities?" wrote Katseba.

"*May the day come soon when you from the East and we from the West shall meet in Germany,*" replied the Englishman. A rendezvous was made over Berlin one particular night so that they might greet one another and thereby please their respective governments.

"Did you see him?" his squadron mates asked on his return.

"Might have," Cheshire replied with admirable disinterest. "Impossible to tell—there were thousands of planes there and anyway it was a very dark night!"

At about this time Cheshire received a letter which now reads very strangely, in view of all the official recognitions of his courage. As a Wing Commander, as has been said, he was not entitled to a crew of his own: so, on each flight over Europe, he took a different aircraft, the captain of that plane then becoming his second-pilot. One of these planes, after he had flown with it, was shot down. In time the captain wrote home from his prisoner-of-war compound to his family: and his mother then wrote to Cheshire.

Her son, she related, had been delighted to observe, on the occasion when he and Cheshire had flown together, that, as he walked to the aircraft, the Wing Commander had also been "scared stiff."

"Don't remember it particularly," the subject of this comment remarks, "but if the bloke says I was, then I suppose I must have been."

With the accumulated risks and disillusionment of almost sixty flights behind him, with the added danger now of strengthened German defences and the increased tempo of war, and with the perpetual worry of an illness which in no way helped him fulfil his duties or his responsibility to the crew with whom he flew, little wonder that he walked across the strip, on those nights, with fear evident in every line of his body. The point is that he walked nevertheless, and flew and bombed and returned. Afraid or coldly fearless, that is all one can ask of any man.

Then, in April 1943, his ill-health was detected and, with a second D.S.O. on his breast, he was grounded. He was elevated to the rank of Group Captain (at twenty-five the youngest at that time ever to achieve such a rank, though Group Captain Dundas later reached it at twenty-three) and given a job, the one he hated and feared most, flying a desk.

Chapter Nine

FLYING A DESK

O N All Fools' Day, 1943, Cheshire went to Marston
Moor to instruct as a Group Captain. He regarded the
day as symbolic and his ground job, as the work of
some sinister hand in Whitehall. This hand, he would maintain
in his more cynical moments, must have belonged to a person
full of a vindictive, discriminatory hostility against himself,
Leonard Cheshire.

In actual fact he knew this was not true. It was merely what
he liked to pretend. He was fully aware of the truth, which was
that his posting was a compliment conferred upon him much
against the will of Whitehall and almost solely because of the
good offices of his friend, Air Vice-Marshal Carr.

Carr was a New Zealander who, remembering his success
with the Halifax squadron, had a high regard for Cheshire as
a pilot and a leader of men. He also saw quite clearly that the
one-time Wing Commander of 76 Squadron was over-thin,
overtired and over-taxed—in short, that he needed a rest from
flying duties. In odd moments of self-honesty Cheshire was
compelled to agree with him.

Nevertheless, without any lack of gratitude to the Air
Vice-Marshal, indeed with every respect for the gusty battle
that worthy had waged with the Brass to secure his appoint-
ment, Cheshire loathed his new job.

For one thing, he knew nothing about it, and he has
always hated, and still does hate, not to know exactly what he

was doing and why. Not, to use his own words, "to know the drill."

For another thing, as he admits, he was "hopeless at administration." Cheshire's leadership has always been by personal example. The iron glove of the martinet, the savage blasts of the disciplinarian, the tearing-off of a strip—these have never been his métier. Rather, he did everything that was humanly possible himself and then relied on others to imitate him. He won friends among all ranks quite deliberately, whether he liked them or not, and then gambled on the affection they felt for him to inspire them not to let him down. Always his leadership has depended upon this personal element of devotion and example.

But there is perhaps little devotion to be won in an office and no spectacular example that can be set from a desk. Cheshire did not consider that wars are won from desks, and even if they were, he said, let others sit at them.

His duties became merely to supervise the training of medium-bomber men on their conversion to heavies. With his invariable good humour he did his best. In his light-heartedly facetious manner he groaned at the never-ending wave of paper work which pounded against his desk. But always he kept his eye open for the moment when those distant superiors, whose edicts he passed on with such dutiful unenthusiasm, would relax their vigilance and allow him to escape the net.

Practically the only diversion open to him at this time was to watch the sales of the book he had written called *Bomber Pilot*. It is an extraordinarily good book. It has sensitivity, imagination and a scholar's ability to choose the right word and yet give no impression of pedantry.

Reading it, one is astonished that a man in whom the qualities of literary fantasy and the ability to see beyond the end of his own nose are so apparent, should have been able to

ILLUSTRATIONS

Cheshire V.C.

Above: Leonard Cheshire, at the age of 4, with his brother Christopher.

Left: Aged 13, after he had shot his first rabbit.

At 17, Cheshire's only ambition in life was to "drive a very fast car round a very curved track and joggle the steering wheel like the race stars did."

Cheshire with a friend, Peter Higgs (right), and a fellow-undergraduate, Jack Randle, who also won the V.C.

Above: Cheshire signing the log book at the Oxford University Air Squadron Summer Camp at Ford, Sussex, in 1937.

Below: Two Cheshires were in the Merton College, Oxford, tennis team in 1938, Leonard (seated right) and Christopher (standing centre).

With some of the members of 35 Squadron, 1941. Left to right: Revs, Brown, Taffy, Hares (at extreme top), Jacko, Weldon, Cheshire, Gutteridge (centre bottom).

Left: "Four days after the wager had been made Cheshire collected his pint of beer from Allen." The *News Chronicle* printed this picture the next day.

Above: "Half the plane's fuselage had vanished." The aircraft Cheshire brought home from Cologne to earn his first D.S.O.

Left: The Gestapo Headquarters in Munich, the Wittelsbacher Palais, was destroyed by 617 Squadron. The rubble has now been cleared, but the bomb-scarred lion remains.

Above: Cheshire and his American fiancée, Constance Binney.

Below: Cheshire with Warrant Officer Norman Jackson at Buckingham Palace after they had both been invested with the Victoria Cross.

Wing Commander Guy Gibson, V.C., D.S.O and Bar, D.F.C. and Bar.

Wing Commander H. B. (Mick) Martin, D.S.O. and Bar, D.F.C. and 2 Bars, A.F.C.

Air Chief Marshal Sir Ralph Cochrane, G.B.E., K.C.B., A.F.C.

Barnes Wallis, C.B.E., F.R.S.

The Gnome-Rhône aero-engine works at Limoges before and after 617 Squadron's raid, February 1944.

"E-boats were pounded and pulverized against the very concrete walls that had been meant to protect them." Le Havre harbour, June 14th, 1944.

Left: The smoke plume billowing 20,000 feet above Nagasaki, after the atomic bomb raid, 1945.

Below: Nagasaki, after the explosion.

Cheshire, V.C., with Wing Commander Nicholson, V.C., and Lord Wavell at Viceregal Lodge, New Delhi.

Right: Sir William Penney, the only other British observer of the Nagasaki atom bomb raid.

In her lovely home at Empshott, Hampshire, near Le Court, Mrs. Cheshire surrounds her son's medals with flowers.

Above: Cheshire with one of the Mosquitos which he flew to Western Europe to build interest in V.I.P. Colonies.

Below: Commandos Benevolent Fund Cocktail Party. Cheshire with Penelope Dudley Ward, Maureen Stanley and Beatrice Campbell.

Above: Cheshire talking to L/C. Todman, R.E., at a foundation meeting of the ex-service Colony scheme.

Right: Cheshire shows patients how to play croquet at his Le Court Foundation Home at Liss, Hampshire. This Home caters for chronically sick young people.

Cheshire in his office at Le Court.

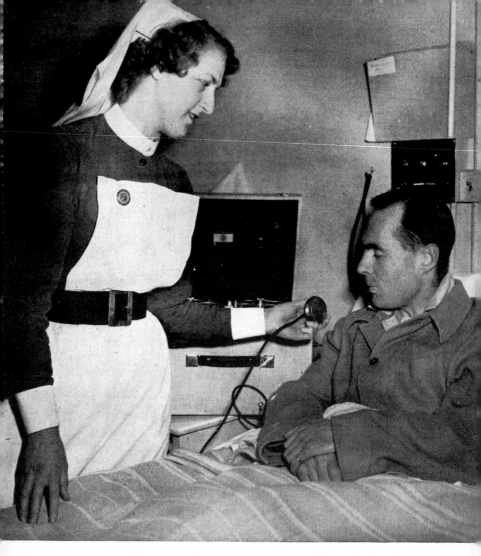

From his bed at the Midhurst Sanatorium, Cheshire records a speech for transmission at Bomber Command's V.C.s' Dinner, February 1953.

Cheshire with Russell Braddon in the grounds of Midhurst Sanatorium.

Above: After eighteen months' illness, Cheshire visits his parents. In this happy photograph he is enjoying a joke with his mother.

Left: Cheshire with his father, Professor G. C. Cheshire, in the garden of his home in Hampshire.

The first time he was allowed to leave the Sanatorium for a week-end, Cheshire visited some of the patients in his Homes. *Above* he is seen talking with 93-year-old Miss Marion Permain.

Below: watching a group of patients enjoying a game of cards.

Left: Lord Tedder laying the foundation stone of the new Cheshire Foundation Home at Le Court, June 1953.

Below: Cheshire viewing the work in progress on the new Home at Le Court.

The Cheshire Bus, equipped to convey his message. This bus is run entirely by voluntary helpers who devote many of their evenings and week-ends to taking the bus to all parts of London.

In the private chapel at Le Court.

close his mind completely to the dangers of operational flying. Bearing in mind the sensitivity of Cheshire, the creative mystic of today, it becomes difficult to see him heading for his target, time after time, with no more emotion than that of George, his automatic pilot.

It is a rare quality, this strong imaginativeness combined with the ability deliberately to freeze one's mind against the pain of unwanted visions. With Cheshire it works not only forward, against those dangers that lie ahead, but also backwards, against those unwanted events that lie in the past. Thus today, with utter sincerity, about many of those facets of his formative years which are now vaguely distasteful to him, no longer compatible with his way of life, he says simply: "I can't remember."

During the war years, however, the quality served him in only one way; to fly and fly and fly. To fly ruthlessly and continuously, to succeed monotonously, to destroy ever more efficiently, and only once, at Antheor, to know a fear so strong that it crippled his purpose and left him helpless to press home his attack in the efficient manner to which he was accustomed.

And he was not aware, even now, of any *mental* need for rest. He still experienced no fear of operational flying, only a vast distaste for the task to which his distinguished rank and his three decorations apparently entitled him.

Wearily he sat behind his files and his telephones and admitted to himself that he was an inefficient devil: wistfully almost he wondered what the boys were doing that night, and whether it was bumpy over "Happy Valley."

He decided that after the war he might become a writer. He was to have a hundred other notions, later on, as to what he might do after the war: but this was the first, and he was happy to think he now had some vocation to which he could turn in peace-time other than the Law.

He followed the course of the war now more closely on the B.B.C. and in the papers. There wasn't much else he could do except fill in 10,000 forms.

There came the massacre at the Warsaw Ghetto, where 56,000 Jews at least were exterminated: the Moehne and Eder dams were bombed and breached by a squadron he had never even heard of, a new squadron led by a pilot called Gibson. Yes, he knew of Gibson.

The Ruhr was flattened: Tunis and Bizerta were captured by the British: Churchill and Roosevelt met in Washington: Wingate cavorted round the jungles of Burma, wreaking havoc on the Japanese: the American war machine swung into impressive action.

"God," lamented Cheshire, "soon it'll all be over."

Sicily was invaded and captured: the marshalling yards at Rome were bombed and Pantellaria captured. In Hamburg 20,000 people were killed and 60,000 injured in one raid, the enemy radar defences having been confused for the first time by the dropping of "window strips." New techniques and new conquests, and still he flew a desk.

Morosely he looked at the airfield around him, standing slim and very straight, his hands on his hips in a characteristic attitude, surveying the rows of planes. He looked like a wealthy young man trying to decide which, of all the expensive sports cars on display, he would buy. Unconfidently he looked at himself in comparison with the men who flew under his orders, mostly older than he, but all his subordinates.

"I've never felt so young," he declared, unhappily. War Commands are not for men who feel young: but still it went on.

Mussolini resigned and was arrested; the British entered Catania; Goebbels announced the partial evacuation of Berlin, and Peenemünde air research station was severely damaged, the enemy's rocket plans against London thereby being delayed six months.

And so, with this last event, although he knew nothing of it at the time, came the longed-for circumstance that was to restore Cheshire to active flying.

The explosion of a German research rocket over Sweden had enabled British scientists to piece together some of the fragments sent over to them, and to reconstruct a picture of the weapon involved. With amazing accuracy they predicted the weight, velocity, trajectory and range of this new and horrific projectile.

Immediately Churchill set into motion all the machinery possible to counteract the effects of long-range rocket warfare upon London. And, at the same time, he demanded that Bomber Command destroy certain strange and astonishingly well-fortified concrete works, now suspected of being rocket-launching platforms, on the other side of the Channel.

The squadron chosen to destroy the five hugest of these platforms was 617, the Dam Busters, of whom Cheshire had so recently read, though he had never previously heard of them. But Gibson, their leader, had gone. And now Air Vice-Marshal Cochrane looked for someone to take the place Gibson had held with such distinction.

At that time Cheshire, tired of his office job, had approached Air Vice-Marshal Bennett for permission to join the Path-finders. Bennett had replied that no jobs were available: and in any event he did not know whether Cheshire was suitable. A trial would be necessary.

Before such a trial took place, Cochrane offered Cheshire the job of leading 617 Squadron and of training them in their conversion from low-level bombing, such as they had used against the dams, to high-level bombing, wherein a huge bomb dropped from 20,000 feet would penetrate below a mass of ferro-concrete and blow up a secret rocket site from within and beneath.

Whitehall were not amused at Cheshire's request for a

transfer from the position of Group Captain at Marston Moor, a position they had granted him reluctantly and only after a prolonged battle, to that of Wing Commander of 617 Squadron. With considerable courage and generosity Air Vice-Marshal Carr, whose string-pulling had secured Cheshire the Marston Moor posting in the first place, now unpulled all the same strings to rid him of it.

Thus, by dropping his rank voluntarily from that of Group Captain to Wing Commander, Cheshire found himself succeeding Gibson to the command of the élite squadron of Dam Busters. In place of the dashing, glamorous Gibson, the squadron now received the donnish Cheshire, slim, quiet and dark, as ever; and with only his irrepressible, bubbling humour to leaven a ruthless determination to go to war.

Chapter Ten

THE LOW-FLYING GAME

THE NEW SQUADRON of Lancasters to which Cheshire now came was no ordinary bomber squadron. It was composed entirely of volunteers many of whom, as he had done, had accepted a drop in rank to join it. It was assigned only missions requiring the utmost precision, skill and daring and was popularly regarded as a suicide squadron.

That this reputation was not undeserved is borne out by the fact that, of the original eighteen pilots who blew up the Moehne and Eder dams, only five survived two weeks after Cheshire took over. Those five quickly became four . . . then three. Those who eventually remained—and who were, with Cheshire, to achieve such astonishing successes—were Shannon, an Australian, McCarthy, an American, and Munro, a New Zealander.

But for some time before their operations began they were, in training, to have the co-operation and advice of a fourth, whom Cheshire has described as "the greatest bomber pilot of the war." That was Mick Martin, another Australian.

The problem with which it was the duty of Cheshire and his squadron to cope was the seeking out and destruction of some of the forty of the original ninety-six flying bomb launching sites in northern France which still survived. Meanwhile a bomb would have to be devised to pierce and shatter the heavy concrete constructions in which the V-1s and V-2s were stored.

The problem had not been left unattended till the last minute by the British and American Governments. Between December 1943 and March 1944 over fifty sites had been destroyed by Anglo-American bombing.

Early war-time dreams he had had on the subject had persuaded Hitler to abandon, or at least slow down, the manufacture of flying bombs and the building of launching sites for some months. But later he authorized both to start again. At the same time 617 Squadron were instructed to attack as many of the remaining sites as possible.

Among the 2,000 Allied airmen who were to die, and the many who flew sortie after sortie to destroy these flying bomb and rocket stores, few achieved such destructive accuracy as 617 Squadron. Before they could achieve the required accuracy they had to invent a new technique, train to it and land a new bomb on a target no larger than fifty yards square, at night.

This bomb was the brain child of a brilliantly inventive "boffin" called Barnes Wallis. He it was who created the special bomb that blew up the Moehne and Eder dams. He had fought a long battle with officialdom to obtain the permission and resources for his special research.

Now, as he had for years, he battled for similar facilities in the creation of a new super bomb, 12,000 pounds in weight, which, when dropped from 20,000 feet, would penetrate any amount of concrete fortifications and, with one devastating, convulsive, earthquake effect, shatter the target from beneath.

He was a kindly-looking middle-aged man with gentle grey eyes and white hair that contrasted agreeably with his pink skin. But an intense strength of purpose and stubbornness of will lay beneath that deceptively mild exterior. Officialdom might not want his bomb, a "tallboy," he called it: they might not see any purpose in it, but the time would come, he was determined, when he would make it.

And so it did. Flying bomb and rocket stores with their threat to London brought permission for him to proceed with his plans for the one weapon potentially capable of shattering Hitler's newest bombing bases.

Applying all his superb inventiveness and tireless skill to the problem, Barnes Wallis went to work. The Nazis were becoming very active across the Channel, and delay might prove costly. With increasing urgency, as the enemy stores grew stronger and more numerous, he worked to achieve success. And whilst he worked Cheshire and his squadron trained to achieve the accuracy required successfully to exploit its tremendous power.

When, by February 1944, this training was ready to be put into effect, it was found that there were delays in providing Barnes Wallis's special bombs. With the squadron fuming at the hold-up, Air Vice-Marshal Cochrane switched them on to high-level *marking* of targets for other bombers rather than leave their peculiar talent for accuracy lying idle.

As a result of these assignments 617's technique of marking targets was again to be radically changed and later, in consequence, the tactics of No. 5 Group's night bombings were to be greatly improved.

The technique of marking and bombing, and the training for it, had marched hand in hand and both owed most of their initial success to the initiative of Mick Martin allied to the unorthodoxy of Cheshire, who allowed his subordinate's suggestions to be put into effect. The need for a new technique in marking the target became most apparent when, after months of training, they bombed as a squadron on a rocket site marked for them at the same height as themselves by a Pathfinder.

In the night operations on these nearby targets the procedure had always been that a specially equipped aircraft marked the target by dropping a flare marker on to it. The bombers then aligned their sights and dropped their bombs on to this flare.

On this occasion the squadron achieved the unprecedented accuracy of dropping *all* their bombs within an average error of ninety-four yards from the marker. But the marker had missed the target by 350 yards. Here, then, was the crux of the problem in destroying targets that were not dispersed but pin-point. The more accurate the bombing, the more accurate must be the marking. Both, in fact, must be spot-on. And with the present Pathfinder technique the marking could not always be relied upon.

Cheshire and Martin put their heads together and prepared the lines of the argument they must present to their immediate superiors, Air Vice-Marshal Cochrane and Air Chief Marshal Harris. These arguments were assembled and expressed by Cheshire himself with that lucidity of thought and economy of language which one would expect from the son of one of Britain's finest jurists and legal writers, and one who had himself, though reluctantly, studied Law.

He pointed out that high-level marking in heavy bombers meant starting one's run-in on the target from perhaps as far away as twenty miles whence any pin-point landmark could well be invisible and must be oblique. Even granted the best of visibility, however, the most skilled high-level bomb-aimers were unlikely to drop their markers with the accuracy required. The oncoming stream of bombers might then drop their explosives three or four hundred yards from the markers . . . and the target would remain unscathed.

Accuracy of marking, therefore, obviously depended upon a low attack, where visibility would be reasonable at least, and where such factors as drift were negligible. But low attacks inevitably involved flying through very heavy hostile fire in the claws of equally hostile searchlights; and to this the ponderous Lancasters would be tragically vulnerable.

Even at 5,000 feet which Cheshire, with his hatred of heights, considered not nearly low enough, a heavy bomber was still not accurate enough and was also extremely vulnerable to light flak. They must fly in even lower and mark even more accurately. Four *hundred* feet was more like it and frequently, in the raids that followed, Cheshire marked at fifty feet from the ground.

Cheshire later summed it up thus: the dropping of markers (those coloured pin-points on the ground which become the actual bombers' only target in a holocaust of flak, searchlights and darkness) is the function of a low-flying aircraft. But Lancasters are designed to function at a great height. Therefore, Lancasters should *not* be used to mark the target: a fast, light, manœuvrable plane should take their place. That plane, added Cheshire, was a Mosquito.

Cheshire is, nowadays, inclined to grin boyishly and brush aside this period of feverish experiments as if it were of no consequence. But it was a time when his nerves were jangled by impatience at the non-stop routine of trial and error.

The need for a Mosquito became grimly apparent after Cheshire and Martin had for weeks been trying to mark accurately by flying in low on the target in Lancasters.

Always, when they did this, they had the same trouble. Their markers landed accurately all right: but, having landed with a flat trajectory, they skidded. Two or three hundred yards they skidded and accuracy no longer remained.

Then, one day as they flew home, Martin spotted a patch of seaweed in the water. Peeling off in one of his spectacular banks, he dive-bombed the seaweed and hit it with a marker that fell more nearly vertically and, therefore, did not skid.

That, then, was their answer. Not to sight and aim at the target with a low approach, but to fly in at a reasonable height, sight the target and dive at an angle of thirty degrees on to it.

A Lancaster, however, is not the machine in which to dive to within four hundred feet of the ground. Something much speedier and lighter was required. Hence their eventual demand for Mosquitos. But many operations were still to be carried out before Cheshire realized that this was their need . . .

Although he agreed in principle to the idea of a new marking technique, Cochrane, mindful of the appalling dangers to a Lancaster of low attack, would not at first allow Cheshire to put their plan into effect.

Eventually Cochrane compromised. But he reminded them sharply of the dangers of marking defended targets from heights which made them vulnerable to light flak. Rightly, despite their impatience, Cochrane insisted that the technique should only be tried out on undefended or relatively safe targets.

They flew off to the Pas de Calais. Flares were dropped from 12,000 feet. Then, as they had determined he should do in advance, privately and most illicitly, Martin had dived thunderously down to four hundred feet, having spotted the target, and had marked it perfectly. His markers did not skid. The bombers dropped their loads dead-on the markers and completely destroyed a huge rocket-launching site. It worked. But in a Lancaster it was a hair-raising business.

Two nights later they went to another site. Martin again dive-bombed, and again the site was destroyed. Their method had now been proved to be no fluke.

Cheshire now went to Cochrane and presented all the facts, except Martin's unauthorized dive-bombing. He begged to be allowed to use the full technique on some authorized target. Cochrane agreed. He selected a lightly defended target in France, the Gnome-Rhône aero-engine factory, and told Cheshire to demonstrate his plan in an attack on that. The marking was to be done by incendiary bombs.

It was a raid which involved risks far greater than the

chance of being hit by light flak. In that great factory worked 300 French girls. The whole area around the target was fringed by French homes. A near-miss might mean sudden death for these people and an unhealthy impetus to anti-British propaganda.

Cheshire accepted the gamble. He flew low back and forth across the factory. The workers quit. He dived from a low height and marked it. The bombs fell precisely on his marker and the factory was utterly destroyed. Only one stick of bombs fell outside the target area and no casualties were inflicted. The gamble had come off. Now for other and better, and more heavily defended, targets.

*   *   *

617 Squadron had now achieved an accuracy such that, from 20,000 feet, they could guarantee two direct hits on any target, 15 per cent of their bombs within twenty-five yards of the centre of the target and 75 per cent of their bombs within eighty yards of it. This was precision undreamt of in the past.

But results considerably in excess of past achievements were exactly those required nowadays to destroy targets that were not vast marshalling-yards or sprawling factories but compact, camouflaged, concrete pens, targets a mere fifty yards square.

Targets had now to be selected with an eye to overall strategy which might not always be apparent to the men in the hangars and the briefing room. But as they worked out tactics and planned each move in the game there was a quiet certainty that every bombing had now to register, no matter how unlikely or improbable the target might appear to be.

Cochrane advocated that 617 Squadron should mark for No. 5 Group. Antheor Viaduct was chosen for their next target, and 617 was regarded as the Squadron with the best chance of hitting it.

The viaduct ran across a bay on the Italian coast, was very

high and only the width of its railway tracks broad. Fifteen thousand tons of supplies for the German forces at Anzio crossed it daily. To destroy it, a 12,000-pound bomb must land closer to it than ten yards away.

When they arrived there, Cheshire and Martin dived down to mark the viaduct. Immediately, the guns opened up on each plane. Both were driven back. Cheshire tried again, and again found the barrage impenetrable. Then, with Cheshire at 4,000 feet deliberately drawing the fire of all the anti-aircraft guns, Martin slipped in low over the hills at the rear of the viaduct. At the last moment, flying through shell bursts and tracer-fire which came at him horizontally, he endeavoured to mark the long, narrow causeway. As he ordered the release of his target markers his plane was hit, two engines were rendered useless, his crew wounded and Martin found himself with a bleeding leg.

"Can you make it back home, Mick?" Cheshire called.

"Not a hope, Sir. We'll try to make the nearest friendly land."

"All right, boy. Good luck." And Martin's plane yawed off out to sea, heading for Corsica.

Cheshire, with vivid memories of the fanatical determination Martin had shown in his attack, now made five more attempts to mark the viaduct. Already his plane had been holed many times. On the seventh attack two shells hit it squarely. There was neither the time nor any more markers nor fuel available for further attempts. The squadron must bomb on the marker he had laid nearest the viaduct, one hundred yards from it.

They did so. Seven bombs exploded within twenty yards of the viaduct, one of them only fifteen yards from it. But the margin needed was less than ten yards. So the attack failed. And with it, for the first time, Cheshire himself was bitterly conscious of a personal failure.

Comparing his own run-in with Martin's, he declared harshly, and with scant respect for the five subsequent attacks he had made alone, that he had lost his nerve. It had never happened to him before. Perhaps, as he considers, it did happen then. Certainly, however, it did not ever happen again.

After this raid Martin had clearly had enough and was sent to 100 Group Headquarters where his great experience could be put to the best use. It was a bitter blow to Cheshire, who unhesitatingly acknowledges his debt to the Australian and who says of him: "I learned all I know of this low-flying game from Mick. I never saw him make a mistake."

*   *   *

It was Antheor which crystallized all the theories he and Martin had evolved into the one sudden, sharp realization that the final answer to their problem was Lancasters bombing at high level and a Mosquito marking for them at low level. This aircraft, because of its speed and manœuvrability, could get in and out through those last, vicious moments of hostile fire such as had thwarted the raid on the viaduct.

Promptly he put his new plan, of marking at the correct altitude *and* in the correct plane, to Cochrane: and Cochrane always receptive of new ideas, equally promptly agreed to think it over.

In the meantime 617 continued their special pin-point raids. An aircraft factory at Albert, a needle-bearing works at St. Etienne, the Michelin rubber factory at Clermont-Ferrand— all were destroyed with a thoroughness unheard of in previous raids. Cheshire's new technique was paying off. Cochrane agreed to try to get him his Mosquitos.

Whilst this was being done Cheshire led further forays. In a vast orange flash, that seemed to bring the sun out of the night-darkened earth itself, the powder works at Bergerac were obliterated by 617's bombs. And another munitions works followed it the next night. On each occasion everyone of the squadron's bombs dropped within the target—damage to civilians and their property outside, nil.

Then Cochrane told Cheshire to accompany him to Air Chief Marshal Harris. They were to discuss Mosquitos.

Harris was impressed. If it was possible to mark a lightly or undefended target at low level in a Lancaster, would it not be possible to mark a defended target in a Mosquito? Cheshire asked to be allowed to attack with his new methods, he was willing to attack the most heavily defended target in Germany.

"Can you do it?" asked Harris.

"Yes," said Cheshire firmly.

"Right," declared the Marshal, without delay. "I want Munich hit. There's been practically no damage achieved there in these past years—not even by the Yanks' daylight raids. So try a dummy run to somewhere as far as Munich and back and tell me what you think about it then. Mark Munich and you shall have your Mossies." He then lent 617 Squadron four Mosquitos and promised that, if the raid were a success, they could keep them.

The dummy run was made on a town near Hanover and it was found that the raid was feasible, although enemy opposition would be furious and the Mosquito would have just sufficient fuel to get to Munich and back—only just. Granted every favourable circumstance of flight and attack both ways, there would remain only a few minutes' fuel in the tanks on landing. Sensibly, Cheshire suggested extra tanks. Meantime, however, the attack had already been laid on, and before those tanks could be fitted the four Mosquitos were due to take off on their first desperate mission. They carried only fifteen minutes' spare fuel. Weather conditions, flak, finding their target and evasive action could easily cost them an extra half-hour.

The four navigators, usually a riotously cheerful group about any operation, were, on this occasion, utterly unenthusiastic. They foresaw, at the best, a future career as prisoners-of-war for the rest of hostilities; but much more probably, it seemed to them, they were faced with certain death. An optimist in the mess, less gloomy than his fellows, suggested hopefully that the trip might be worth a week's leave when they got back.

" *When!* " muttered one.

"Fat lot of use that will be to us," added another.

They flew to Manston airfield, the closest possible take-off point to Munich, and parked their planes on the runway to save fuel, even for taxi-ing. Then, sombrely contemplating their frugal reserve, they marched off in twos to the crew room.

To Shannon, a fellow pilot, only one other flight with Cheshire had ever seemed as foredoomed as this. That was an unauthorized dropping of Christmas presents that Cheshire had planned for his brother's prisoner-of-war compound. Shannon and Martin had both been persuaded by Cheshire to join the project but both had been unashamedly relieved when an Intelligence Officer had convinced their leader that the dropping of gifts would undoubtedly be construed by German sentries as the dropping of arms: and that any who picked them up would be shot. It had seemed a pretty desperate venture. No one, except Cheshire, was sorry that it had to be abandoned. Now they were to attempt an even more desperate mission. As they walked to the crew room Cheshire pointed out that there was a beautiful sunset.

"I'm not interested in beautiful sunsets," snarled Shannon, "I'm only interested in beautiful sun*rises!*"

This made Cheshire hoot with that characteristic unexpected and delightful laughter of his. He laughed because the mordant national wit of his Australian colleagues always tickled him, and because, apart from Martin, he had never met anyone so utterly unafraid of anything as Shannon. So, back-chatting amiably, they left the strip. In the time that remained to them before take-off the four pilots and their four navigators, each to his own fashion, withdrew into his own thoughts.

Cheshire's thoughts were far from gloomy. Though acutely intelligent and creative he was not unduly imaginative about dangers that lay ahead. He had the capacity to shut out of his mind anything unpleasant and, since nothing is more unpleasant than the anticipation of extreme physical danger, he now disregarded it completely.

So, instead of contemplating the probable failure of their fuel supply on their return from Munich, or the likely destruction that lurked for them among the forest of ack-ack guns which protected that city, he thought cheerfully of the days he had spent in Germany before the war.

And thus the time passed until they took off. Then there were no further moments for reminiscing. Each pilot strained every nerve to avoid destruction: each navigator sweated over every landmark and over every breath of head-wind. Their destination was Munich, *and back*. Their objective, to mark a target more accurately than ever before so that it could be bombed more destructively than ever before.

As soon as they were away from Manston, Cheshire and his navigator, Pat Kelly, settled down to deal with vile weather conditions. Tentatively Cheshire fingered the belt he wore round his waist. He had had it specially plaited from sixty feet of unbroken silk parachute cord. He reckoned that if ever he were shot down no one who captured and searched him would be suspicious of a mere belt. And, if he were locked up and still had it, sixty feet of silk cord might be very useful in an escape attempt. Wryly he thought that never had the prospects of his using this belt been more lively than tonight.

He thought of Taffy and Willy and Christopher, all now

prisoners in Germany. His mouth tightened, losing all its deceptively prim softness when it did so, at the thought of Christopher. His brother's capture had made the war a very personal affair for him. After a school career that was only average and a University Second instead of the First expected of him, it had added to the triumph of doing something supremely well, the fanatical urge to end the war quickly and so secure his brother's release.

Again he fingered his belt. He had no sense of carrying a mascot. Didn't have much faith in mascots. Look at Desmond's wireless operator . . . worse still, look at the little grave on the squadron grounds that belonged to Nigger.

Nigger had been the immortal Gibson's mascot dog. Nigger had been killed. Now Gibson must fly without a mascot, with only a neat little grave as a reminder. It was a very respected plot of earth on the squadron and today it is hallowed as a memorial to Gibson's gallantry and the squadron's reputation. Mascots were no use. You needed luck, not mascots. You either had luck or you hadn't. He was glad he had it, particularly on this flight.

Below lay thick cloud *and*, they hoped, the Rhine. Above, unbroken and as high as 17,000 feet, was more cloud. Cheshire decided to break radio silence and ask Shannon how he found the weather. But instead of Shannon's voice there came back other unmistakably Australian accents, which he recognized instantly as Martin's: "Is that you, Sir?" Martin asked—Martin whose experiments had led equally with his own to this very raid.

"Is that you, *Mick*?" Cheshire called back. "Where on earth are you?"

"Oh, I'm around." Cheshire grinned to himself. He *would* be, he thought. He had known that Headquarters wouldn't hold Mick for long.

"What the hell are you doing?"

"Sticking my neck out for you types!" came the answer. He was beating up night-fighter fields to forestall attacks on the incoming British bombers.

"One of the intruder boys," Cheshire told himself, grinning again. Good old Mick. Then, not wishing, by further conversation, to provide enemy plotting stations with a "fix," he signed off.

"Good luck to you, Mick."

"Good luck to you, too. Be seeing you."

And Martin's wishes of good luck were not unavailing. Almost immediately the cloud vanished and dead on time they hit Munich. So far, then, none of that precious reserve of fuel had been wasted. The flare force had arrived in advance, bathing the city in pitiless glare, and the defences were already spitting up a hell-fire of defiance. A hundred searchlights remorselessly sought out the intruders.

Cheshire called out: "Marker leader going in . . ." and peeled off from 10,000 feet. Always, in practices, he had been terrified of being struck by one of the few flares dropped from above him to illumine his target area. Now he dived at an angle through hundreds of them, not to mention a bubbling fizz of ack-ack, with never a qualm about any of them. He was silhouetted by flares from above and spot-lighted by searchlights from below. The ack-ack seethed round him.

(*"How do you account for this sudden lack of fear?"* he was later asked.

"I don't know," he replied. *"Too busy, I suppose. Anyway I assure you I never gave flares or bombs or ack-ack a thought. Makes it difficult to assess courage, doesn't it?"* he added phlegmatically.)

He was required to mark a particular house some hundred yards east of the main railway station. To the west were two lakes, which also served as landmarks. In the clear, flare-lightened night he had easily spotted his target and now screamed headlong down towards it. The tiny plane twisted against the turn, complaining at this unwonted speed that rose and rose and buffeted by the near misses of exploding shells. Gently Cheshire coddled his aircraft into a true, plummeting flight, grateful that it was a tiny Mosquito and not a cumbrous Lancaster, and the house hurtled up towards him.

With sheer will-power he fought off the instinctive, fear-laden urge to bomb early and flatten out. Not until the last second did he press the button on his control column and then ease the stick back. As the screaming plane straightened out of her dive Cheshire, and Kelly beside him, became dizzy with the relentless pressure of gravity; then their eyes cleared and they were hurtling flat over the roof-tops of Munich.

Swiftly he climbed above the flares, rolled over on one wing and looked down for his markers. Wickedly they glowed back up at him, two baleful red eyes that would mean utter destruction to the nearby railyards when the other Mosquitos had marked and the two hundred Lancasters had bombed on them.

Cheshire now flew round Munich, disregarding the tiny reserve of fuel available to him, and personally directed the bombing of 617 Squadron's Lancasters. Mostly this was done with code words; occasionally, though, under the stress of excitement, the code would be forgotten and plain language used. At only 1,000 feet Cheshire flew immediately *below* the path of the falling bombs. About the possible danger to himself of this practice, he announces blithely: "The risk of being hit in an aircraft by a falling bomb is very, very slight."

Yet, in his own squadron, one of the Lancasters had suffered precisely such a hit from a falling bomb, fortunately only a small practice one. He must have known of the incident and that the risk was not nearly so slight as he has declared, with his usual understatement.

617's task competently, as ever, fulfilled, Cheshire at last decided—Kelly had long since decided the same!—that they had been floating round Munich long enough, and they should now set off for home. Gladly Kelly gave him a course. Relaxed after the tenseness of the raid, a spectacularly successful raid, which for the first time had hit this target, they flew through the night.

Now that the task was done and the danger over, Cheshire and Kelly, as they always did, lit cigarettes. This they did cheerfully and with no compunction at all, even though there was danger of petrol fumes from the Mosquito's inside tanks filling the cockpit and though the practice was expressly forbidden by regulations. Companionably they sat side by side, tearing joyfully through the night, and smoked.

Then, without warning, the joyousness and the tranquillity vanished. They were suddenly trapped by searchlights and for the next forty miles could shake off neither them nor their attendant flak for a second. For twelve awful minutes Cheshire sweated . . . and tossed the small plane round in violent evasive action, the solace of his cigarette forgotten. Pat Kelly, powerless to help, swore lustily throughout.

Typically, Cheshire found time to spare a thought for his companion, who had nothing to distract his attention from the murderous dangers of the ubiquitous flak. He decided that a navigator's job was much more frightening than the pilot's. The pilot should mostly be too busy to be frightened although, he confessed frankly to himself, he was frightened now. One was not keyed up to this sort of thing *after* a show like Munich. He cast a compassionate eye at the cursing Kelly and he would have been even more compassionate had he known that, in a later raid, this navigator was to be killed.

Then, just as suddenly as it had started, so it stopped. They now flew to Manston in peace, which they knew to be assured. Their only worry thereafter, they knew, was fuel. Their gauge said ten minutes' reserve: but one never trusted gauges when they read as low as that. "Ten minutes" could equally well mean that their tanks were empty. But soon Kelly saw Manston below them and the last of their cares vanished.

"What's wrong with the runway?" demanded Kelly suddenly. "Look at those funny lights." So Cheshire, who had flicked on his navigation lights preparatory to landing, looked, as they dipped down towards the flare-path, at Kelly's "funny lights."

Abruptly he realized what they were—the flashes of an enemy fighter shooting-up landing aircraft. Cheshire was angry. Not even now was Danger prepared to let them slip through her fingers. For the second time since the actual raid, when, if life were just, all should have gone smoothly, they were gravely menaced.

He was doubly angry because he had grown accustomed, on their home airfield, to the friendly protection of a neighbouring fighter squadron. It wasn't exactly an official protection, rather the result of his own charm and ability to get things done for him by other people. As an isolated and vulnerable bomber squadron this amiable protectiveness on the part of the fighters towards 617 had been most welcome. Now, on his first landing away from the squadron, an enemy fighter awaited them, and he with his navigation lights on.

"Turn those bloody navigation lights off," Cheshire snapped. "It's a Jerry fighter."

Kelly had before him a neat array of switches. In his excitement he turned them all off. Thereupon, as Cheshire himself commented, "everything packed up." For a few wild seconds there was uproar. It required all his strength of mind and skill to overcome this last hurdle. Then they landed smoothly and climbed stiffly out of the cockpit and went to the briefing room.

They were home. All the Mosquitos were home. Home, having initiated a startling new technique of bomb marking:

home, with less than fifteen minutes' reserve of fuel in each plane: home, with the proof at last that the Mosquitos could fly in and mark very low without being hit.

For Cheshire the raid had been a personal triumph: to his companions it was just the same old "bloody war."

"Wake me," Shannon instructed Cheshire, "at sunrise. I want to see it!"

Chapter Eleven

EARTHQUAKE BOMB

B Y personally leading his squadron against Munich in a
manner never employed before, and advocated only by
himself, Cheshire vindicated all his theories about
accurate bombing being the twin function of marking the
target alone from low level and then having his Lancasters,
20,000 feet above, bomb on his marker.

Of this new technique in bombing he recounts: "The Air
Force world in general were against us." But that was only at
first. After the early French raids, both the American Air Force
generals, Spaatz and Doolittle, visited Cheshire to find out
how such extreme accuracy was achieved. He explained in
his usual clear but matter of fact style, and the Americans took
away with them an impression of ice-cool efficiency.

There were inevitably detractors of both Cheshire and the
new low-marking technique. Cheshire himself was quite unmoved and completely disinclined to look back upon the
crushing raid on Munich. Bigger bombs and more devastating
raids were now being actively scheduled.

And whatever certain critics thought of 617, Air Chief
Marshal Harris had no doubts about what had been achieved.
After Munich he reorganised No. 5 Group and gave them a
squadron of Mosquitos and two squadrons of Lancasters, to
act as their own marking force. 617 were given four
Mosquitos of their own.

Unfortunately, at this time, Barnes Wallis's bomb was still

not ready for the squadron, so that their attacks on the rocket sites were again delayed. They now, therefore, began the most intensive training project the squadron had ever known. No one in the squadron could imagine what purpose lay behind this incessant practising because none of them could imagine how their intricate and split-second manœuvrings could possibly be fitted into the general pattern of the war.

Yet the operation which involved them in such arduous and monotonous training was, in fact, to be their contribution to D-Day. The squadron, by complex manœuvring and circling over the Channel, in which an error of only four seconds in timing could wreck the whole plan, were, at twelve-second intervals for almost six hours on end, to drop bundles of "window" in steadily advancing waves. This, it was hoped, would lead the German radar erroneously to detect an "invasion fleet" where, in fact, there *was* no invasion at all—only falling strips of silver paper. They rehearsed it for weeks.

Because of their perfect precision and impeccable discipline they were successful. The Germans confidently anticipated landings at Cap d'Antibes and Calais, their radar having located these fleets that were merely ghosts. Meantime the real invasion landed at Normandy. Of this invasion 617 Squadron saw nothing. Their rôle was invaluable and safe. But they did not enjoy chess games even if their own particular move had helped to tie up a great enemy force until it was too late to cross the Seine and join the real invasion.

For the first time in the war 617 had objected strongly to an assignment.

"Do what you're told," Cochrane instructed Cheshire unsympathetically. And so the invasion had started and, with it, Hitler's desperate fling of a rocket war against London.

*   *   *

It was at this stage of the war that the curiously divergent mentalities of German scientists, Hitler, Cheshire, Cochrane and the English "boffin" Barnes Wallis were indirectly but jointly responsible for a series of 617 Squadron's most sensational exploits.

The German scientists at Peenemünde had invented and constructed rocket-propelled projectiles which would carry a ton of explosive across the Channel to Britain. For a considerable time, as has been stated, Hitler's chance dream that they would not succeed had caused him to deny the Peenemünde scientists the priorities they needed for their planned production of three hundred rockets a month.

Then Major-General Dornberger met Hitler and showed him a film of the new rocket, known at Peenemünde as the A-4, at work. Fifty or sixty miles it rose into the air; one hundred and sixty miles away it hit the ground again with an appalling explosion. Hitler forgot his past dream and instantly superimposed a new one upon the reality.

"Produce *two thousand* a month, not three hundred," he ordered, "and let them carry *ten* tons of explosive, not one." Both were impossible and Dornberger told him so: but Hitler did not hear him, obsessed now with his own vision of this new wonder weapon.

"Call it the V-2," he decreed. "Vengeance Weapon 2." He moved restlessly round the table on which the plans for the rocket lay.

"Europe and the world are too small from now on to contain a war. With such weapons humanity will be unable to endure it." Humanity has heard the same about gunpowder, gas, air forces, blockbusters, atom bombs and H-bombs, and still, in its madness, it endures them all. But this was Hitler's V-2, his own brainchild (he was convinced of that now), and V-2s would crush Britain and end the war.

"They are only long-range artillery," Dornberger demurred.

He knew V-2s could not win the war. But Hitler ignored him.

"*Ten* tons of explosive," the Führer demanded. "What I want is annihilation. The annihilating effect."

Dornberger told him they would be fired from mobile platforms, hard to detect and always in a different place. But, as Dornberger himself mournfully relates, Hitler's favourite project nowadays was the construction of vast, concrete shelters built by slave labour: so the Führer over-rode him and decreed that they should be fired from permanent sites, massively fortified, to be built in Holland, the north of France and the Pas-de-Calais.

So the sites were built and detected by Allied reconnaissance. The rockets were ordered into mass production and the source of their manufacture passed on through Intelligence to Whitehall and Washington.

Then Peenemünde research station and the factories of Friedrichshaven and Wiener-Neustadt were put out of action, as were most of the sites, by Anglo-American air raids.

Fresh reports of the secret weapon, and the photographs of the concrete stores, now spurred the Allies to plan counters. One very essential move was a new bomb that could destroy these storage works and factories immune from ordinary bombing. Another counter was the training of aircrew to drop such a bomb on precisely the one position where it would achieve its effect.

Barnes Wallis invented the bomb. Cheshire trained and led the squadron whose task it was to lay the tallboys not *on*, but *alongside* the target.

Cheshire and Barnes Wallis shared a genius for unorthodox, sometimes brilliant, sometimes impracticable, ideas: Cochrane had another kind of genius, that of being able instantly to sift the two lines of approach and to put into effect those plans which were of value.

Barnes Wallis's bomb, to be effective against Hitler's twenty to thirty feet of concrete fortifications, needed not to hit the site directly but to strike immediately alongside it, bore deep into the earth and explode beneath it. Then the "quake" effect would shatter the concrete from below and around, as no blow from above could ever do.

And in May of 1944 this new weapon, 12,000 pounds of lethal, shark-like, sleek bomb, became available for 617's use. Since January the squadron, after five months of training in Cheshire's hands, had been ready to use it. Now stocks of them arrived. And within forty-eight hours of their arriving, 617 Squadron put them to use. Cheshire led the squadron and, dive-bombing from 5,000 feet, laid his marker dead against the Saumur tunnel. Within minutes the tunnel and the mountain itself through which the tunnel passed had been devastatingly collapsed by the tallboys that fell on and through them. The bomb did everything that Barnes Wallis promised of it.

"We nursed it, patted it and did everything one might be expected to do with a baby *except* show it off," Cheshire relates of the tallboy after it arrived. "We alone, of all the Allied Air Forces, now possessed the equipment and the bomb capable of destroying the five monstrous launching platforms that the Germans were building in the Pas-de-Calais."

Accordingly, within days of the first flying bombs falling on London, in June 1944, Cheshire led his squadron against the two main secret weapon installations, the massively fortified Hitler favourites at Wizernes and Watten.

Accurately marked at about four hundred feet by the Mosquitos flown by himself and Shannon, both were destroyed by Barnes Wallis's tallboys, which fell 20,000 feet from the squadron's eighteen Lancasters flying in above their leader.

"God help the Jerries," Kelly remarked compassionately to Cheshire as he saw the destruction of Watten, and the target vanished in a haze of dust and rubble. They smoked more soberly than usual on their return trip home. What a bomb this was. And how accurately now they could lay it.

Then Cheshire asked for an American Mustang instead of a Mosquito. The Mustang was faster and even more manoeuvrable than the British plane and he felt certain that he could mark for his squadron to even better effect in one of these aircraft. The ever-generous Americans provided one promptly. And within hours, in a new, single-engined fighter-plane that he had never flown before, without a navigator (the fighter accommodated only a pilot) he led another attack.

He had to act as his own navigator, pilot, bomb-aimer and wireless operator. Yet such is the ferocious application of the man that, in sixty minutes of practice, he mastered sufficient of all these diverse arts to fly with confidence and lead a brilliantly successful raid on the flying bomb launching and storage site at Siracourt.

He put his markers within a few feet of the huge concrete, ground-level roof: and immediately the tallboys blew up and sealed off the entire store. Henceforth he always led his squadron in the Mustang.

The little plane would pierce in low and alone, hurtling through a barrier of shrapnel. Then it would dive at thirty degrees and drop its marker at the last second, flattening out to skim the earth and the guns that fired at it so angrily. As the marker glowed or smoked the bombers would snarl in, high, deliberate, ominous. Down would crash the earthquake bombs. Huge concrete blocks would crack and totter. The site would collapse. Then the little Mustang and its giant companions would turn triumphantly back towards England.

Less then half the projectiles manufactured by the Germans were ever fired. Because the heavy damage inflicted on Peenemünde held up research, less than twenty per cent of these rockets were sufficiently perfected to reach their target in England. Though the rocket war lasted from June 1944 until March

1945 it never succeeded even in impeding or delaying the Allied invasion, still less in crushing it. Bomber Command had strangled Hitler's dearest weapon.

By July 1944 Churchill could report in the Commons that 50,000 tons of explosive had already been dropped on flying bomb sites and other rocket targets: and that many thousands of reconnaissance flights had been made to seek out the skilfully camouflaged "ski-sites." Up to the day that he spoke 2,754 flying bombs had been launched: only 2,752 fatal casualties had been sustained.

"I am sure of one thing," Churchill concluded, "that London will never be conquered and will never fail, and that her renown, triumphing over every ordeal, will long shine among men."

So the invasion continued, Churchill's report being both a message of defiance to Hitler and of London's stout-hearted self-confidence to Eisenhower.

Altogether 9,000 V-1s were launched against England: only 6,000 reached even the coast. Fifteen hundred V-2s were launched and the casualties they inflicted made each one of them negligible in value in comparison even with each of the small Mosquitos which attacked enemy Europe.

Such was the fate of Hitler's wonder weapon. It was eventually rendered impotent when those few remaining launching sites and storehouses not already bombed out of existence were captured by the Allied reoccupation of western Europe.

But, until that final moment of impotence arrived, the weapon created by German scientists and exploited by their Führer was ruthlessly sought out, in its own theatre of operations, by Cheshire's squadron, under the control of Cochrane, using the "earthquake bomb" invented by Barnes Wallis. Men's fates and characters become curiously interwoven by wars!

*   *   *

Altogether, Cheshire personally led 617 Squadron on some forty raids. He was invariably its spear-head. Yet the measure of his wartime achievement is not to be found in his raids or even in his brilliant inventiveness and leadership. He was always prepared to back his own judgment and events proved him right time and again. It should not be forgotten that the low-marking Mosquito squadron which joined No. 5 Group had easily the lowest casualty rate of all in the Group.

Antheor was his only failure, if it can be called such. As against that, he arrived at 617 knowing it to be the élite, volunteer squadron of Dam Busters : he left it, a year later, as his own élite volunteer squadron of high-level, precision bombers. Gibson made the squadron famous for the breaching of the Eder and Moehne dams : Cheshire added to its reputation by the destruction of flying bomb dumps, rocket sites, powder works, aero-factories, railway tunnels, and E-boat pens.

Each raid was a miracle of determined accuracy. The Saumur tunnel, for example, had been collapsed by a bomb which fell on the mountain above it, pierced sixty feet and then blew up exactly inside the tunnel itself, hurling 10,000 tons of rock and rubble into the air.

At Le Havre they scored another resounding success. It was June 14th and the invasion was going well. Nevertheless, the Allies had no great desire to allow E-boats to sink their supply . ships, so the pens were to be attacked. The whole of Groups 1 and 5 were mobilised for this tremendous raid.

Flying a Mosquito again, instead of his Mustang, Cheshire took off just after nine o'clock at night. It was still light and the presence both of a navigator and an escort of Spitfires, a rare luxury, gave him a strong sense of security. This would be a good raid and it was the first in which the Mosquito marked by day.

The attack on the port area would be made in two waves with 15 Mosquitos, three of which would mark the target should his own markers miss or be extinguished, together with 325 heavy bombers.

As he reached the coast he pushed the little plane down and hurtled in through a curtain of ack-ack to the heart of the harbour. And there, fatally tied up in the neat concrete bays, were 15 E-boats. Cheshire felt himself surge with exultation at the sight of these sitting ducks which could be anything but placid on the high seas. Not only would they blow up the concrete pens, but most of those E-boats should go west too.

No amount of ground fire could deter him now, not with a target like this. Down, deadly accurate, went his red flares. Overhead, in the gloaming, protected by Spitfires, his massive Lancasters droned in. Then tallboy after tallboy smashed down on to those twinkling spots of red that were his flares. As the pens caved in, the water in the docks and all the harbour boiled and exploded and E-boats were pounded and pulverized against the very concrete walls that had been meant to protect them.

The total shipping destroyed that night was 53 boats of various kinds. And of the E-boats only one remained servicable after this raid.

On to Mimoyecques. Fantastic gun-barrels, designed to pour six hundred tons of explosive daily into London, were sunk five hundred feet into the ground. This target, only thirty by twenty yards square from above, was swiftly marked, bombed and buried.

Creil, in a huge cave near Paris, a vast store of rockets and buzz bombs was collapsed and sealed off by No. 5 Group.

Calais, another store was entombed inside the chalk hills.

Two days before this Calais raid Cheshire had been asked by the Intelligence Officer at Woodhall Spa how he felt about the fact that he had now completed ninety-eight raids, that he should now, statistically speaking, have been killed at least four times.

"You don't feel the strain, Arthur," Cheshire told him. "You keep on going, more or less automatically, and don't worry."

Now he had flown one hundred missions. A hundred times he had gone out, bombed, endured ack-ack, fought fear and tiredness and cold, exerted all his skill, exploited all his ingenuity, and come back.

In four different squadrons he had seen all his colleagues— or almost all, it seemed—die or go missing. There were no secrets about himself left to him, nor any illusions about war: and no smallest part of the art of destruction was now unknown to him. He had forgotten almost everything in life except leading his squadron, setting an example of frozen courage in every attack, bombing, shattering and killing the enemy.

When he thought about this at all, which was seldom, he considered it an excellent thing. He was fine-drawn and taut as a violin string. Though he had lost not an ounce of his skill or daring, his eye twitched often and he did not know it.

Cochrane called him over to Group.

"I see you've done a hundred trips now," he said. "That's enough. It's time you had a rest."

Cheshire roused himself to protest but the Air Vice-Marshal forestalled him. "It's no use arguing," he told him. "A hundred's a good number to stop at." And then, as if to soften the blow to this brilliant, startling and unconventional Wing Commander through whom he had achieved so much, he added:

"Shannon, Munro and McCarthy will come off too."

So the three surviving Dam Busters (apart from Martin) and

the man who put low-level target marking on the map left the distinguished company of 617 Squadron at the same time.

Though this seemed the end of his career, life was just starting for Leonard Cheshire.

Chapter Twelve

FLASH-BURN

TO MARK his achievements of determined leadership and courage over a long period, the King now invested Cheshire with a third D.S.O. and the Victoria Cross. In addition he was restored to his rank of Group Captain. Now, for the fourth time in five years of almost continuous combat, Cheshire attended Buckingham Palace.

The Victoria Cross was awarded not for any one particular action but for a prolonged series of them. The citation at one stage reads: "During his fourth tour, which ended last July, Wing Commander Cheshire led his squadron personally on every occasion, always undertaking the most dangerous and difficult task of marking the target alone from a low level in the face of strong defences." It went on to state, for example, that "in June 1944, when marking the target in the harbour at Le Havre in broad daylight and without cloud cover, he dived well below the range of the light batteries before releasing his marker bombs and he came very near to being destroyed by the strong barrage." The citation concludes: "Wing Commander Cheshire has now completed one hundred missions. In five years of fighting against the bitterest opposition he has maintained a record of outstanding personal achievement, placing himself invariably in the forefront of the battle. What he did in the Munich operation was typical of the careful planning, brilliant execution and contempt for danger which has established for Wing Commander Cheshire a reputation second to none in Bomber Command."

Cheshire's V.C. was the hundred and fourth of the war, twenty-one of which had gone to the R.A.F.

He tells of his investiture in his customary bland and casual manner.

"It's all a bit vague now. I remember I went in first and the King stood on a dais with a whole lot of important-looking people behind him. He was very gracious. Had an uncanny knack of saying just the right thing. Anyway, when I was through I had to wait at the side of the room until everyone else had been decorated. I hadn't been there long when some-one in Court dress came up and whispered: 'Would you like a drink?' So I said I certainly would. He gave me the sign to follow him.

"Well . . . we walked up and down stairs and around corners and along about eight hundred miles of corridor" (Cheshire's figures are always multiplied by a delightful schoolboy exaggeration) "and then we arrived at a sort of hatch thing in the wall. This courtier bloke knocks on it, a very secret knock, and the hatch opens. From then until the investiture ended I drank bottles of Guinness and nattered with the King's butler!"

In spite of this diverting anecdote, however, Cheshire had a deep respect and loyalty for his King and the Royal Family. "I've been lucky enough to meet them five or six times," he says, "and it always moves me very profoundly."

So much for his award of a Victoria Cross. About the decoration itself he says: "Please, when you're writing, give due credit to all of those who *deserved* V.C.s and didn't get them. You see, unless an action is highly publicized *and* successful it's very difficult to get one. But lots of blokes earn them in unpublicized or unsuccessful actions, specially in the Army. Anyway, *my* V.C. was given to me, not for anything I did, but for all of 617 Squadron. Lots of other chaps in 617 deserved them more than I did. Shannon, for example. And

Mick Martin had a complete genius for low-level attack." He paused to choose his words, and then added deliberately: "You see, blokes like Shannon and Martin pace you, you've got to keep up with them. My colleagues all acted as my pacers."

"And it was a one-way pacing only, I suppose?" he was asked sarcastically. He gave the old familiar hoot of laughter.

"Think what you like," he replied, "so long as you write what I say."

For a few months Cheshire enjoyed a well-earned rest, and during that time realized, from the degree of his pleasure in that rest, just how severe a toll the war and its waging had taken on his body and nerves. But, from the very beginning of this vacation from combat, Cheshire had had no intention of lying back in healthful idleness. Always the bars of Mayfair had been his leisure-time occupation. Now he had much more leisure . . . and the bars saw much more of him.

"Glad to see you're properly dressed at last," a young Flight Lieutenant in the Ritz remarked to him on one such occasion, pointing out the ribbon of the Victoria Cross that shone newly among all his other decorations. He had been Cheshire's bomb-aimer and was entitled to the familiarity. Cheshire grinned self-consciously and moved on.

"Congratulations," said Alf, his favourite barman in another bar.

"That's Cheshire, he's just got the V.C.," a group whispered among the cushions in yet a third. Doggedly he drank in all his favourite haunts. Then came a discordant note in this alcoholic jaunt. Someone, in one of his most beloved bars, was talking about God and what God was.

The subject was incongruous and the thoughts expressed were muddled. Like most men who have faced death often, Cheshire had very decisive and very unmuddled views about God. He interrupted firmly.

"God," he declared, "is your conscience which tells you right from wrong or good from bad." He had spoken with all the authority of a Group Captain and the awful, aged wisdom of one who has lived to be twenty-six through the worst fires of a war.

Then came the shock. "Nonsense," a woman's voice contradicted. "And I'm surprised that anyone in your position should say anything so stupid. God is a person."

In a bar . . . by a woman . . . what's more, a woman who drank there as much and as often as he did himself . . . late at night, and glowing with alcohol, Cheshire had astonishingly found himself verbally assaulted about, of all subjects, God! The thing was so incongruous that it stuck. For days he found himself wondering which of them, himself or the woman, was right. Characteristically, not being sure on the matter, he decided to find out! As upon every other subject that he came up against, Cheshire *had* to know the drill.

Before his theological investigations had gone very far, he found that the Air Ministry were becoming increasingly interested in his future. Hostilities in Europe had ceased but, as a London paper enigmatically reported, "a number of gentlemen with much experience of dropping things on Germany are now moving out East."

One of these experienced gentlemen (indeed who more experienced or gentlemanly?) was Group Captain Cheshire, V.C. He had been offered any job he liked and asked for the Southeast Asia assignment because that seemed the most likely way to get back on to operational flying. So he moved out to Burma, on to the headquarters of Eastern Air Command, South-East Asia, as a legendary figure. He moved out cherishing twin but ill-assorted ambitions: to know more of God and to destroy more of Japan. But before he had been long in the East, events occurred which moved him to America.

Because his wife was ill at this time she had to return to the

United States. A sympathetic administration allowed Cheshire to join her, relieving him of his duties in Burma, and so he landed in Washington.

Once he was there it seemed a pity not to make use of him. Accordingly he was attached to a United Kingdom Mission whose task it was to liaise with the Americans on all branches of the common war effort. Cheshire was required, as an Air Force representative, to attend to the matter of tactical weapons.

"Very interesting too," he declares, and then hastens to add, before anyone can start asking awkward questions, "not that I can remember much about it."

Nor can one find out little about *him* at that time either. Two witnesses give the following reports of Group Captain Cheshire as a member of a Military Mission.

"Couldn't get to know him at all. Rather aloof and shy."

"Talked too much. I thought he was a bit of a line-shooter."

Since each nullifies the other, and since Cheshire either can't remember or won't talk, one must rest content merely with the information that for a short time, which included a miserable holiday during which his wife was thoroughly unwell, he stayed in Washington.

His stay was terminated by an order to present himself to Field Marshal Sir Henry Maitland Wilson.

"*Field* Marshal?" Cheshire queried. "But that's the Army." If it had been the Russians it couldn't have seemed odder to him.

"Good Lord," he moaned, "what on earth have I done now?"

So, full of apprehension, he went off to see Field Marshal Maitland Wilson.

The reason for the summons, it turned out, was not any grave breach of Army discipline on his part but an instruction by the Field Marshal, acting as the representative of then Prime Minister Mr. Attlee, that Cheshire should proceed at once

from Washington to the Mariana Islands in the Pacific there
to work with the American Air Force on a special mission.

He packed quickly and flew out of America. Leaving Washington and his wife, with whom he was never reunited, he
approached the turning point of his life.

On the fateful day when Field Marshal Maitland Wilson
invited Cheshire to go to the Pacific he, in fact, invited him to
attend, with Dr. William Penney, the dropping of the Allies'
newest weapon upon Japan.

Atomic bombs, product of British research and all the
incredible laboratory and industrial wealth of the United
States, were to be dropped on both Hiroshima and Nagasaki.
Cheshire and Penney were there to observe the explosion over
Nagasaki.

So he departed to the Mariana Islands which the Japanese
themselves had triumphantly occupied during the war and
since lost back to the remorseless ocean campaign of America.
He went to assist his allies on a project that was to be the
turning point in the lives of both himself and of humanity.
Momentarily, in the wild enthusiasm of learning about this
strange, new weapon, he abandoned his questionings about
God.

Ironically, the very cause of that abandonment was itself
to be the greatest cause of his subsequent much more serious
pursuit of the subject. Nagasaki, for the first time in his career
as a bomber pilot, brought home to him the conflict, inherent
in war-making, of killing and Christian ethics.

"Did you ever feel any compunction about your bombing
raids during the war?" he was once asked.

"None," he declared firmly. "Over Germany one was much
too busy most of the time thinking about the technical process
of hitting the target and evading ack-ack to consider what
might be inside that target in human terms. When one did
think of it in human terms one remembered the blitz and all

the shocking things the Nazis had done, and one felt no compunction. Matter of fact, I rather enjoyed it.

"As for Japan, this bomb was obviously a very big one and the more big bombs dropped on Japan in the shorter time, the sooner the war would end and save many more lives, both Allied and Japanese, than any mere air-raids could destroy."

He considered the whole matter of bombing, his chin resting on those long fingers in his characteristic attitude. Then he delivered his own bomb-shell.

"As a matter of fact," he declared, "I may as well confess that we were so keen on dropping this bomb on Nagasaki, and would have been so disappointed if the war had ended without our doing so, that some of us jokingly suggested, if Japan *did* surrender before we flew to Nagasaki, that we might even fly there and drop the bomb just the same!"

So much for any sense of conscience Cheshire may have had about being party to atomic warfare before the event. It was rather with boyish enthusiasm and the coldly determined thrust and leadership of one who, in terms of sheer personal achievement, could almost be described as the most destructive man of the war, that he flew off on that historic August morning in 1945.

And so he reached Japan, comfortably and in unaccustomed silence, in shirt sleeves, without an oxygen mask, at 39,000 feet, at four hundred miles an hour and in conditions that in terms of speed, height, aircraft and crew discipline, were all utterly foreign to him. It was a summer's day, hot and cloudless, and the sky was blue. He put on his welder's glasses and looked out towards the unsuspecting city that seemed to drowse unwarily in the sun's fresh warmth. He looked out and wondered what would happen below them.

And below them, as the two silvery, ephemeral aircraft droned lazily towards Nagasaki, the not very efficient Japanese

Air Raid Service issued an alert and later, almost immediately, relaxed it. In the two valleys that forked into the heart of the city about 100,000 people lived poorly and worked stolidly, in their national fashion. On the other side of the city another 160,000 dwelt and worked. The whole town was about as big as Portsmouth.

Then suddenly the faint rhythmic droning of American engines, so different from the erratic harshness of their own aircraft, was heard . . . and three parachutes dropped lazily . . . and men and women looked upwards curiously.

There came a bright flash in the sky and many shut their eyes at its brilliance. Others kept them opened . . . and in a few seconds the bright flash built up within itself a heat so incredibly radiant and vicious that their eyeballs were savagely seared into blindness.

Then the ball of fire above them belched out a haze of white smoke which roared downwards at them and the summer day darkened unnaturally. There was a sense of wind and heat.

Directly under the blast, the skin on exposed Japanese turned crisp black: farther away, clothes were flash-burned, all the coloured parts being eaten neatly out of the white material of shirts and kimonos.

Tiles bubbled with heat: metal and stone surfaces lost their smoothness and became instantaneously corroded. Where workers or pedestrians had stood between these surfaces and the greedy lick of a flash that came from an immeasurable ball of fire, macabre shadows of their outline were left unscorched on the otherwise pitted material. The humans themselves vanished, charred to death so that their negative might be eternally and uselessly etched on stone or mineral.

Trams and buses for a few miles around were destroyed, and the people in them. Wooden houses burst into flames. Screaming citizens fled from a horror that no ordinary bombing had inspired in them. Officials and rescue squads fled with them. Injured Japanese, trapped in buildings that had been first crushed by blast from above, then squeezed inwards by pressure at the sides and finally torn apart by a blast of suction as the heat waves cooled off . . . these injured lay helpless and unable to move whilst slow-growing fires incinerated them.

All the crops and vegetation for 2,000 yards vanished, leaving only blackened earth.

Five hundred and eighty workers crossing a bridge were burnt to a man. In a concrete hospital the walls and ceiling withstood the blast but the woodwork caught fire—and half the occupants died.

Almost all of the wooden-housed factories of the Mitsu-bishi clan, in the valley, caught fire or collapsed. Workers were crushed, burned or blasted to death.

In this the most ancient centre of the faith in Japan, the scene of the greatest massacres of Christians in other centuries, the Roman Catholic Cathedral was blasted into a shell and then set on fire. Everywhere steelwork buckled, walls blew out-wards, roofs were dented downwards, woodwork ignited as if by magic and the town rocked as though in the grip of a vast cyclone.

All this happened in one ten-millionth of a second, then passed, leaving only ghastly silence. A silence broken by the crackle of flames, the moaning of the injured and the far-off, faint, rhythmic droning of two American Super-Fortresses.

In the next two weeks thousands were to go blind, to start vomiting, to suffer a form of bloody diarrhoea, to succumb then to anaemia, internal bleeding and infection. Altogether the deaths continued for about eight weeks. Of the 100,000 directly exposed to the bombs in Nagasaki, some 40,000 died: 60,000 of the total population were left completely homeless and 25,000 inadequately housed. This happened in seconds. In the *whole* war only 30,000 Londoners were killed by air attack. An atom bomb, even an inferior one like that dropped on Nagasaki, can now be relied upon to kill 50,000 in any city: a German V-2 rocket on an average killed only fifteen. Thus has science progressed.

These are the things the people of Nagasaki saw on that day when Cheshire looked down from 39,000 feet and saw the writhings of an atomic explosion over what remained of their city.

And though none of these things could then have been known to him, as he watched the writhing cloud, obscene in its greedy clawing at the earth, swelling as if with its regurgitations of all the life that it had consumed, Cheshire suddenly sensed it all. In one monstrous ten-millionth of a second his mind revolted against everything that this cloud implied. The same flash and blast that killed 40,000 Japanese curdled all desire in him to kill again. There must, he realized, be better things to do with one's life. There must be some power higher in the universe than that of nuclear physics. There must be something that he personally could do.

In that split second of nuclear fission came the greatest moment of truth in his life. Now and inevitably, Cheshire, the supremely efficient man of war, the much decorated hero of one hundred mortal raids against the enemy, became Cheshire, crusader for peace.

Chapter Thirteen

V.I.P.

UNABLE to endure the prospect of further visitations such as Nagasaki and Hiroshima, and faced with the promise of a land war little less mortal, the Emperor of Japan now ordered his subjects to lay down their arms. Reluctantly, and unconvinced, all over South-East Asia, they did so.

Only in Burma, at the hands of the British XIVth Army, and in the Pacific and China Sea Islands, which had fallen to the Americans, had the Imperial Japanese Army experienced defeat. In China and the Malay Archipelago were hundreds of thousands, even millions of Japanese soldiery whose war had been one long, spectacular triumph. Now, at the behest of their Emperor, they left the arena. And so World War II, it was said, ended.

With this abrupt termination of hostilities a new Cheshire emerged. The youth that he had hoarded and put aside for six long years now reasserted itself. But it did so upon a man whom, inevitably, war had moulded. Consequently he became, and is today, a curious amalgam of aged experience, youthful frivolity and spiritual maturity. He is a product that only war could bring forth: he was one of those rare personalities so equipped, mentally and spiritually, that he could become that product.

To many ex-servicemen his character, with its affinity to their own sympathies and antipathies, is easily understandable:

to many a civilian he is an enigma: to others of both strata he is merely "round the bend."

To some degree he invites this last description. Since 1942 he had always revealed a streak of erratic brilliance. As the years passed he became more and more the originator of a steady stream of new ideas. Some, as he admits frankly, were terrible. That is not the point. The point is that he committed the social crime, in this world, of having original ideas; and he added to it by reviving his Oxford-days' determination to be different. To be original is bad enough: to be different is unpardonable. Hence . . . Cheshire is round the bend.

But to analyse this madness. In 1943 he decided he would like to write for a living after the war. In 1944 he told the King, at an investiture, that he would like to study geology. Next he decided to take a colony of picked comrades to a remote island and settle there, away from the squalor of world politics. This gave place to a plan for growing mushrooms in a disused tunnel (disused installations have always had a fascination for Cheshire). Later he suggested to Martin, Shannon and Munro that they should form an experimental aviation company.

"Air travel removes national boundaries and nationalism," he said. "It links the common man of one nation with his counterpart in another and they find that they, as individuals, have no axe to grind." His proposed colleagues accepted this profound thought without undue worry. They were accustomed to Chesh's profound thoughts.

"Also," he declared, "we might finish up flying to the moon."

"He's off again," the three of them thought to themselves; and the idea fell through. That was in 1945, when any mention of flying to the moon was decidedly a symptom of dementia. Now, of course, it is generally accepted: Americans are already staking claims to properties up there in their own home towns: Cheshire spoke of what is today a commonplace. But *then* he was "round the bend."

After this he took to practical, non-sectarian Christianity; communal living, international ideals.

Now he has become a Roman Catholic and has created four Homes for the chronic sick and the aged, Homes which are inspired by his own personality and depend for their existence upon that inspiration even more than they do on the businesslike management of the various committees which today run them.

In none of this would there seem to be a trace of "round the bend-ery."

All young men and women, of any intelligence at all, on some occasion or other decide that they would like to write. In the destructive environment of war the creative urge to write is wholly reasonable, especially writing of the type Cheshire enjoyed, a playing with words and a delight in fantasy.

The island colony was a more explicit development of this desire. Mankind is pretty difficult to benefit *en masse*. It appears to be stubbornly averse to being helped and much more inclined to be destroyed: therefore one must experiment with a small and chosen band who *wanted* a better life and a better spirit in it. The sort of spirit one had always known in the Services, for example, and so seldom met outside. Why not perpetuate it?

Mushrooms could easily have been the outcome of a yearning all battle-weary warriors experience just to see something grow: and equally of the desire of all those about to re-enter civvy street to make a living, but *not* in a pit, and *not* only a pittance.

His aviation plans, experimental and visionary, speak for themselves. Behind them the sensitive recognition that here was a means of bringing men together, even of extending our known universe.

And so to a more Christian way of living. His various post-war projects of colonies, homes and religious crusades . . . all of them inspired by the one thought: that civilization had turned itself into a frightful mess, everyone should do something to get us out of it.

It will be noticed that behind all his plans, erratic or otherwise, there is the one common motive, a creative desire to improve or restore. Nowadays one can look to statesmen and see in their international dealings only futile and despondent haggling: one can look to many of the established Churches and see only dull ritual and sectarian squabbles: one can look to scientists and see only bigger and better bombs.

For all his faults, and he has the normal, human quota, one prefers to look to Cheshire. He, at least, is getting something done and always planning a jump ahead of events. To understand the prophetic insight of the man, read again what he said about the atomic bomb in 1945. Note the year: others, with awful and ponderous authority, are saying it now, but Cheshire uttered these words nine years ago.

"I myself am not a scientist and I do not understand nuclear physics. To me the words and figures that these atomic scientists use so freely, even in casual conversation, are just words and figures. They have no meaning. I cannot visualize time in terms of millionths of a second nor heat in terms of tens of millions of degrees.

"Before this flight I could not conceive of a man-made flash that would illuminate the cockpit of a plane fifteen miles away in the full light of the sun. Neither could I conceive of a ball of fire twenty-five times as large as the Ritz Hotel rocketing up into the atmosphere five times as fast as the fastest jet fighter in the world and, at the same time, dragging the very dust of the ground up with it.

"None of that could I conceive, and yet now I know that it is true, because I have seen it happen. I have seen, too, the ball of fire transform itself into a huge luminous cloud that seemed almost possessed of some evil, lifelike quality, as though it were a shapeless monster of the deep convulsed in its agony of death.

"To conceive that all this can happen, means changing your fundamental concept of what is possible and what is not possible. It is a problem which the mind cannot easily solve, and for that reason the human mind is apt to turn away.

"The facts of what the bomb achieved are now commonplace among the world. We know, in approximate figures, that the blast effect was equivalent to the simultaneous explosion of 20,000 tons of high explosive; that the heat was the same as the internal heat of the sun and that the flash was several times brighter than the sun.

"We know, too, of the destruction and death that it caused and we know that by bringing the war to an abrupt end it saved more Allied lives than it killed of the enemy, a fact in itself which should confound the argument of those who complain that the use of the bomb was an offence against humanity.

"The physical effects of the bomb can be reduced to facts and figures; they can be sifted and sorted and shown to the world. But what the world cannot be shown, and therefore cannot visualize, is the fantastic proportions of the spectacle itself.

"I had been as fully warned of what to expect as was possible from verbal description. I had lived with the men who had built the bomb; I had seen it in component parts; I had touched it, talked about it, and thought about it.

"In spite of this I was still not prepared for what I saw.

"It was not that the explosion was different from what people said it would be, but purely that it was so unbelievable in its proportions. *When Wilhelmshaven blew up we felt a sense of elation. We had set out to destroy and we had destroyed. When Nagasaki blew up we felt nothing but an overwhelming sense of awe, not because an unusual number of Japanese had been killed but because something had happened which altered our fundamental concepts of life.*

"About the future there has been much conjecture and much speculation. From the confusion and uncertainty, however, there emerges one fact which we should do well to grasp and digest.

"Atomic energy is a stern reality and is not in the realm of religion or magic. It is a staging post along the road of scientific knowledge and is not a secret locked in the bowels of the earth which may either be uncovered or hidden at the will of man.

"*Scientific knowledge is the property of the world and not of nations. It is not a physical possession like territory,* and therefore cannot be denied or withheld except by denying the right to carry out research. Its progress cannot be halted any more than the development of industry or of medicine could be halted.

"*In other words atomic energy will very shortly cease to be the exclusive property of England and America.* We do not possess the power to withhold it from other nations, nor to decide who will have it.

"*Today it carries the power of victory,* because, so far as we know, no one else possesses it. *Tomorrow,* however, when the whole world possesses it, *it will not in itself carry the power of victory any more than high explosives did a year ago.*

"It will merely carry the power of destruction over an unprotected enemy which will be immeasurably greater than anything we have previously known."

One month after the war ended Cheshire, publicly and without leaving himself any discreet loopholes through which to escape the grave responsibility of his words, made this statement to the Press. At the same time Western statesmen were talking and thinking only in terms of a wonder weapon which would, by its deterrent effect, keep the peace for many years. If this is their peace—let them keep it! But these are not his only warnings.

In November 1945 he stated, apropos of Anglo-American discussions: "The necessity of ending war is a biological necessity. It is a choice between survival and extinction.

"At this moment, while the big talks are going on in the United States, we are faced with this straightforward and plain issue: if we should ever fight another war, we have lost everything we ever had.

"There are three courses before us. They are:

"To rule out the possibility of war; or

"To send the whole nation permanently 1,000 feet below ground; or

"To abandon this country and disperse its people throughout the Empire." Cheshire believed it impossible to accommodate 50,000,000 people underground, to employ them there, entertain them there and enable them to travel from one place to another underground. Describing the bomb, he said: "Heat developed was around 10,000,000 degrees and the light of its flash several times brighter than the sun.

"*That bomb was a very small one.* Its percentage of efficiency was very small. *Any future bomb produced will be very much stronger.*

"*I think that the figure of* 100,000 *times as strong is not very far off the mark.* If ever there is another war these bombs would destroy every city we have."

Thus boldly did he predict the American advances at Bikini, the British explosion on Monte Bello, the H-bomb itself. How many others in 1945 declared forthrightly: "I think the figure 100,000 times as strong is not very far off the mark"?

And again in November, on Armistice Day, he wrote for the Press: "I witnessed, only a few weeks ago, the total extinction of a city and of most of its inhabitants.

"The Japanese who once lived in the city were my enemies and I had good reason to wish them harm. My purpose in visiting them that sunny August morning was to kill; indeed, my whole business in life was to kill; and therefore I should have been satisfied at having killed so many in so short a space of time.

"When it came down to the point, however, not even the enormity of the spectacle, nor the certain knowledge that the war against Japan was over, was enough to obliterate the horror at so vast an extermination.

"If the area of destruction at either city were superimposed on the map of London, and centred on Piccadilly, the outside of the circle would cut from the north of the Zoo down through the Angel, the Mansion House and the Elephant and Castle, across Kennington Oval and the far side of Chelsea Embankment and up to the western edge of Kensington Gardens.

"Within that circle there would be nothing left, except ashes, rubble and the Thames, to show that London had ever existed—and the labour of almost 2,000 years would have been undone in one ten millionth part of a second.

"If you think that this is a little far-fetched, or that this is not a proper topic for Armistice Sunday, *then you have already taken the first step along the road that the last generation took. You have not faced up to the facts.*"

At the beginning of 1946 Cheshire's retirement from the R.A.F. was announced. Instantly a series of interviews with the national Press followed. Cheshire mentioned his desire to study for subsequent scientific work.

"Not that I have any training for it," he remarked happily, "but I think that we are coming to a very interesting time and I should like to understand something about it."

"In our lifetime," he continued eagerly, "we are going to reach the moon. With the use of atomic energy, the deserts will become habitable." Cheshire considered a moment how best to tackle this vast field of science.

"I am playing with the idea of studying geology first," he declared.

In a later interview he explained his retirement, a cause of mystery to all. "I am extremely sorry to leave the service, but it is what I want. I joined as an amateur, and it is different in peace-time. One needs a lot of detailed knowledge which I don't possess and I don't think I am really suited to being a peace-time officer." Remembering his horror of cockpit drill and his constant conspiracies against authority one must agree with him in this.

"Like a lot of other people, I went straight into the Air Force from school. Now I think I shall spend the next ten years acquiring an education, learning something which will eventually fit me to take a job in one of the sciences, probably geology or physics."

Asked if ill-health compelled his retirement, he parried with that admirable vagueness that always afflicts him when his physical condition is discussed. "Not really. It was just that when I got home from the raid on Nagasaki I was a little tired and they put me in hospital for four weeks."

And a week later, showing no signs at all of ill-health or tiredness, indeed writing with brisk vigour, he declared:

"If we, as a nation, are to maintain our position of power, we need to go out into the world and sell the English doctrine. We need to play our part in fortifying the Empire and so show the world that no matter what the job might be we can do it better than anyone else."

It is only now, a decade later, that Britain begins to feel the same.

At the end of 1946 he declared bluntly: "Of the British Central Control Commission in Germany there is little to be said that stands to their credit. The damage they have done will take many years to remedy." Seven years later, the premature arrest of alleged neo-Nazis by British authorities was to prove him sadly right.

"The armed forces," he went on, "are very different. If ever democracy should succeed in establishing a foothold in Germany it will be due to them."

In March 1947 he said of the German people that they were, he sensed, waiting for something. Was it, as it had been after the last war, a leader? He could not say, could not define it. But this he did say . . . "the more I see of Germany, the more convinced I am that, beneath the outward semblance of law, order and co-operation, there is an undercurrent—and that one day, if we are not wary, the undercurrent may become a flood."

He added: "Under a convincing cover of good-will . . . vengeance, hatred and greed are rife." Cheshire's reactions to other peoples' emotions, whether overt or covert, have always been astonishingly sensitive. This statement, unequivocal as it is and was meant to be, may well turn out to be a prophecy of the Bonn Government using a new-granted German Army to play West against East for her own ruthless aggrandizement. Nothing would surprise Cheshire less.

Of the men and women who served during the war, he had this to say: "Those who went more or less straight from school into the war have been brought up on the highest and most impelling motive that life can offer. *Now they must be content with one that is far inferior.* Furthermore, they are starting their careers later in life than normally they would have done, and because of that they cannot easily afford to start at the bottom. They have grown up on a spirit of adventure. Under wrong direction the spirit of adventure is harmful both to the individual and to society. Under right direction it is an asset."

And then, in April 1946, he remarked caustically: "Strength

is once more measured in terms of guns, efficiency and dollars: the weak are still at the mercy of the strong, *and we are already on the way towards another war.*"

Quite naturally, foreseeing as he did the nature of this other war, not a year after the last, admiring the spiritual strength Britain had shown in 1940, rather than her fawning dollar-mindedness of 1946, frankly nostalgic for the cheerful camaraderie of service life, rather than the class bickerings of peace-time, and, above all, obsessed now with the truth and validity of the Second Commandment, Cheshire turned his back firmly on organized, State-planned society and sought to set up colonies of his own in which men would lead a better and more enjoyable life. In his colonies he hoped to foster, under right direction, all that spirit of adventure which had recently been so extravagantly demanded of, and so generously granted by, the youth of the late 1930s and had apparently gone for so little gain.

Here, then, were planted the first seeds of his war experiences, of his restless urge to do something and of his new-found conviction that the world must, to survive, turn to a Christian way of life. As ever he appears to have anticipated a world movement by almost a decade. Today the Abbé Pierres and Billy Grahams of our civilization preach the same gospel to huge followings of ordinary men and women.

The first seeds died, but the idea was right: and, undeterred by an initial failure, Cheshire was to move on from it, developing his ideas and changing his methods, becoming that rarest phenomenon today, an ordinary man who has broken through the inertia imposed on their citizens by post-war governments, who has dispelled the apathy of the "What's the use? What can *we* do?" school and has put into effect a series of projects that are creative, altruistic and practicable.

*   *   *

The colony scheme, which failed so completely, started with the issue of a challenge to ex-service personnel. Cheshire asked, through the Press, why they should not form a group who would again live the communal life they had known so well, each contributing a lump sum of cash as backing for the project, each working within and for it according to his own trade or profession, and each then receiving a weekly payment of £4.

"We will take over a disused aerodrome," he suggested, remembering that there were hundreds of them, "or any other suitable estate, and move into it. Our first task will be to make ourselves self-supporting, for least of all do we want to live on charity in any shape or form. Whatever we lack in skill or resources we will make up for in hard work and unity.

"Therefore we will farm and cultivate the land and carry on any productive industry that lies within our power. When that is done we will create an organization to train those who need it in their own particular trade. We will use our pooled endeavours and knowledge not to make our fortunes but to help each and every member to set himself up in life to his best possible advantage.

"The experience of war has taught us that there are qualities and talents in all men which everyday life never gave a chance. These we will exploit by every means within our power, for we believe that every man can give of his best when there exists the same kind of fellowship and spirit that existed in 1940 and in all the past moments of national danger."

The challenge was promptly accepted by some 200 enthusiasts. There were officers and rankers, men and women, of all three Services. Meetings were held and ways and means devised. The weak fell out and the others grew more enthusiastic. Finally, in a large forty-five-bedroomed house near Market Harborough, the first colony started.

Soon another sprang into existence in a house of twenty-five rooms that Cheshire had bought very cheaply from an aunt of his, a house called Le Court. In the meantime Cheshire himself flew in a private Mosquito to various parts of western Europe to build interest in what he hoped would become affiliated colonies over there. They might even found a colony in South America, he suggested. They would become truly international, linked by radio, aviation and a universal fellowship of interests.

But they failed. They failed simply because, as well as the service spirit, there was also a service-like administration— nasty little typed notices and a constant atmosphere of Standing Orders and rosters. They failed equally because there was no incentive for the individual to succeed spectacularly in his own trade, since all profits were pooled.

The colonists were human. They did not mind contributing their share: but they did not wish to contribute one cent more than that share. If they earned more, they had to pool it: therefore, either they did not earn it or they resented bitterly paying it into the pockets of others. Conversely, there were those others who were not in the least averse to doing nothing and being supported by the rest.

Nevertheless, the failure was gradual and the lessons to be learnt were incessant.

In November 1947, explaining the creation and present condition of his colonies (known as V.I.P. or *Vade in Pacem*), Cheshire declared that he had conceived the idea out of two convictions: One, that the only personal security left in a world of squabbling, class-conscious governments lay in friendship with the ordinary men and women who surrounded you; and, second, that the only physical security left in a world of rapidly swelling atomic arsenals lay in the dispersal of the world's peoples into small, self-supporting groups. He went on to detail the progress of his own ventures.

"We have faced bankruptcy twice," he declared blithely. "We have more than once reached the point where it seemed utterly futile to continue any further. We have made more mistakes in a year than I should have thought it possible to make in a lifetime. But now, at last, we are enjoying a temporary rest from misfortune and I am leaving soon for Canada to arrange our first V.I.P. colony overseas."

Typically, Cheshire did not give the real reason for his visit to Canada.

Worn out by the war and the constant rush of his first post-war years, he had been ordered to go overseas and relax. For six months he rested in Canada and also worked in a lumber camp. Between times, he conversed frequently with his host, an ex-Bishop of Korea, on the subject of religion. He still had no specific faith, except that of a Christian way of life and the necessity, by word and example, of preaching it: but if these conversations did not greatly mould his opinions at the time, at least they stimulated him to further research later on. Restlessly he cast around for what, to him, would be the final answer.

Then came the news that his two colonies in Britain were not only devoid of funds but hopelessly in debt. Promptly he returned to England to surrender what little remained of his personal wealth and then to work in order to pay off those thousands of pounds of debt.

So V.I.P. foundered and vanished. Cheshire was left with nothing but the ideal that had inspired it and the bills that resulted from it. He clung undeterred to the first, paid off the second and then, enthusiastic as ever, set off on new ventures.

Chapter Fourteen

TRUE OR FALSE?

ALL OF THE original seventy colonists, except two, a Colonel and Mrs. Weddell, had left Le Court within five months of Cheshire's return from Canada to pay off the tradesmen's accounts and multitudinous other bills and to wind up the scheme.

He roamed the large house restlessly, conscious that the presence of two other people merely aggravated its emptiness and apparent futility. Then he had word that one of the ex-colonists, a man called Arthur Dykes, was gravely ill and wanted to see him.

Dykes had been moved from Le Court during one of Cheshire's regular visits to Holland. He had gone there to lend his support to Churchill's United Europe Movement. When he returned he heard that Dykes, suffering from cancer, had been taken into Petersfield Hospital.

Dykes, or Arthur, as Cheshire prefers to remember him, had come to Le Court because his mother's death had left him alone in the family cottage and his health broke down when, having left it, he went to work on a farm. As an ex-I..A.C., the colony scheme appealed to him.

Now Cheshire went to see him in hospital. The matron explained sympathetically that the man was incurable and that there was no more they could do for him. She hinted, too, that his bed was needed for another case to whom medicine could hold out some hope.

Knowing the facts, and the man, and knowing that, though he was not afraid of death, Arthur was greatly afraid of all the medical mystery which so clumsily surrounded his person, Cheshire maintained that Arthur should be told the truth. He argued so persistently that eventually the doctors agreed, and Arthur was told, though by whom Cheshire can no longer remember. "Probably did it myself," he decided. "I know I felt very strongly on the subject."

Since the hospital wanted his bed, Cheshire tried desperately to find somewhere congenial for the old man to go instead. He had a horror of a dying man ending his life among people who had no particular or personal feeling for him.

With his customary vigour he approached everyone of any influence.

"I pulled every string I could think of—Benevolent Fund— everything under the sun. But it didn't work."

Then he saw Arthur and spoke frankly to him.

"I'll take you home with me to Le Court," he offered. "It's up to you, if you'd like to risk it." Arthur said he would like to risk it.

Cheshire collected him in his own car, drove him to Le Court, put him into a bed made up with borrowed linen and blankets, having himself carried the man into the house and up the stairs, distempered the walls of the room, rigged up a makeshift bell from the patient's bed to his own room and then settled down to a new life.

At last he had found a good use for Le Court. For the next few months he was to act as nurse, companion and friend to the ex-L.A.C.

There was only one moment of panic. On the first night the bell champed and clattered frantically. Waking out of a dead sleep Cheshire found himself full of cold fear. "My God," he thought, "it's a hæmorrhage or something. I haven't a clue what to do."

He rushed into Arthur's room full of terrible expectations.

"There's a cat come in the window," the patient complained mildly. "Please put him out, Len." Cheshire put him out and the crisis was past.

"Life became very full after that," he said. "When I wasn't looking after Arthur, or cooking meals, I was scything the grass. It grows you know." He rubbed his forehead wearily as he spoke: and one felt that, though grass grows everywhere, in no place does it grow so relentlessly as it did at Le Court.

"At night we used to talk a lot—very strong R.C., Arthur was—often discussed religion—and then Arthur would read a bit, always seemed to be the same book, and then it'd be time to turn in, ready for the next day."

The weeks passed and Arthur, though he grew weaker each day, came to feel more and more at home. With the aid of vegetables that he grew and sold, and food sent over by an ever-attentive mother, Cheshire managed to keep both of them alive, well fed and warm.

About nursing, he learnt as he went along, always being quite cheerfully prepared to ring up the local hospital and ask advice if any snags occurred. And with Arthur in the big old house he at last felt he was getting somewhere, putting his ideals into practice. Once again he had a mission in life, to make the last weeks of a fellow serviceman happy and comfortable.

Shortly after that the porter at the block of flats in which one of Cheshire's aunts had lived remarked on this nursing eccentricity of the good Group Captain's to an elderly friend of his. The friend was himself an invalid and possessed a bedridden wife. The next thing that Cheshire knew was that the wife, aged ninety-four, arrived at Le Court on a stretcher and asked him to accept her into his home. Promptly he did so.

Curiously he looked at the new arrival. Le Court was growing! She was fully dressed and wore her best hat, complete with a spectacular feather. Cheshire was most impressed by the feather.

"Funny way to be dressed when you're on a stretcher," he thought inconsequentially, as the bearers carried her up to an empty room. They deposited her carefully on a bed and then looked at Cheshire to see what he would say. He could think of nothing to say. All he could think of was the feather in the hat. They grinned at him and tipped their caps.

"Thanks very much," they said.

"Thank *you* very much," Cheshire replied, and so they departed, leaving him with his second patient.

Swiftly and somewhat apprehensively he made enquiries from the local hospital as to how one nursed patients who were not only ninety-four years old but bedridden and female as well. They told him. Washing, it seemed, was the most vital treatment.

"All over?" asked the momentarily appalled Group Captain.

"All over," they replied firmly. So up he went to her room to wash the old lady all over.

About the removal of most of her clothes she was quite indifferent, and about the washing. But on the subject of her woollen socks she was adamant. They would *not* come off, she declared. "They never 'ad."

"Well they've got to now," Cheshire told her, and the battle commenced. Every night for a fortnight the same Battle of the Socks was fought. And every night for a fortnight, when he had won the battle and washed the old lady all over, he would ask kindly:

"Now, how are we tonight?"

"Awful," she would reply, briskly and without fail. "I want to go home." And then, as a last thrust, she would demand: "I want me cat. Where's me cat?"

Every night for a fortnight and then, on the fourteenth

night, when he asked her the routine question, after the usual battle, she opened her mouth to blast him, closed it again and announced:

"Very well, thank you. You know, I love you," and flung her arms round the neck of her truly astounded nurse. "I love you, too," he muttered amiably, and from that day onwards he had no further trouble with her, not even about her socks.

But soon after this Arthur died. Cheshire sat up with him all night and Arthur awaited his death with calm and composure. Occasionally he read his book. Then suddenly he was dead and Cheshire felt very lonely without him. He took Arthur's book away with him to read because he knew that sleep was impossible.

"I felt at a loose end when the old man died. You see I'd been nursing him day and night. The only other things I ever seemed to do were scythe the grass and tear off Grannie Haynes's socks. Then suddenly I didn't have to look after him any more: and even though the grass still grew and had to be scythed, and Grannie had to be looked after, I felt at a loose end. So I started reading Arthur's book.

"It was called *One Lord, One Faith*, by a man called Vernon Johnson, a very famous Anglican convert to Roman Catholicism."

The book, it seems, was his apologia: and it told Cheshire the Roman Church's case as he had never heard it before, which was, simply, in a way that he could understand.

This was a most exciting event for Cheshire. From 1945 to 1947 he had endeavoured, without a formal faith, to lead a Christian life and to promote it by means of V.I.P. Then, for six months, he had worked to pay off the debts of that experiment. Now, in mid-1948, he suddenly found a Church putting a case which he could not only understand but with much of which he agreed.

What was more, the case was put without any equivocation.

It left itself no loop-holes. It laid down rules and laws and dogma: and there would be no deviation from them. It had authority and, to one who had lived an active-service life for six years, authority seemed essential in any system that was to work. It was clear-cut and unevasive and to him, whose mind was half legal and half a smoothly-geared instrument of war, that was good.

"It was good," he told me, "because either everything it said was true, or everything it said was false." As he spoke, he held his hand up vertically in front of his face with the edge of the palm towards his nose. At the word "true" the hand and forearm swung sharply to the left: at the word "false" they swung sharply to the right. It was a curiously ecclesiastical gesture, and yet equally the gesture of an ace bomber-pilot describing a bank either to port or starboard.

"There could be no half way in their case," he said. "So I thought . . . well, if it *is* false, then there must be one very good reason *why* it's false. I shall ask all the Anglicans I know what one very good reason they have for declaring the case of the Roman Catholic Church to be false."

Here he smiled. "Well, they did all have one very good reason. And they all seemed to become extraordinarily worked up when they gave it. And the reason was always very violently posed. The trouble was, everyone gave a different reason. And, worse than that, most of them cancelled each other out.

"For example, one said '*they won't move with the times*'. another said '*they always keep adding new doctrines to catch up with the changes.*' The only common complaint, and this decided me more in favour of the Roman Church than against it, was '*Well, look at the sort of people R.C.s are, and look at what they do.*' "

More confused than anything else by all this reasoning, Cheshire then approached a Roman Catholic priest, told him about the book he had read and asked for advice.

"You'd better read the Church of England's reply to *One Lord, One Faith*," the priest advised.

"Its arguments were strong, brilliant and numerous," Cheshire states, "and completely above me! They just didn't register."

So he remained more than half-convinced that the Roman Church's case had stood the test. To decide the matter he asked Father Henry Clarke for instruction. He wanted to know all "the drill." The priest was reluctant but Cheshire was persistent. Eventually he won bi-weekly instruction over a period of four months: and he was received into the Church on Christmas Eve of 1948.

*　　*　　*

By the time of his reception into the Roman Catholic Church Cheshire had eight patients and a staff of two. And by the Christmas of 1949 he had thirty-two patients and a much larger staff, also quite a deal of the medical equipment needed to look after so many invalids.

How did he get so many patients? Alan Finch, the present warden of the Home, answers the question very simply. "He just took in anyone who knocked on the door." He took in people of all ages and various complaints. Some were old and helpless, some were crippled, some had nothing wrong with them whatsoever and some were tuberculous.

They paid what they could—if they would!—and voluntary donations and local hospital schemes made up the balance of the moneys required. From the very beginning Cheshire, neat and tireless in his white coat, refused to worry about finance.

Cheshire allowed no criticisms or vicissitudes to deter him, and there were plenty of both. When household equipment was needed and there was no money to buy it, he scavenged in local dustbins and dumps, bringing back old brooms and bits of timber. When things broke or fell down in the ugly old Victorian house, he mended them himself and hoped for the best. When patients were ill all night, he sat up with them. He had only one aim in life, to make all his residents feel that they were leading as normal a life as possible and that they were at home, not in a Home.

To this end he encouraged those who could to work and to contribute to the running of the establishment. He exerted his undeniable power to get people to do things for him and, both inside and outside Le Court, he had dozens of devoted supporters.

But it was not only individuals who succumbed to the remorseless Cheshire charm. So improbable an institution as the South Western Regional Hospital Board undertook to meet the cost of sixteen of the patients: local welfare authorities paid up with unwonted amiability for the support of others: the Church Army gave him his first substantial gift, £200 worth of furniture. Voluntary Labour also arrived from such unexpected sources as the Royal Academy of Dramatic Art.

It was not in his character, however, to let others do the work and himself sit around issuing a steady stream of orders. The man who, as 617 Squadron's commanding officer, had failed, day after day, to use the car that waited outside his office and, upon eventually being rebuked by a hurt W.A.A.F. driver, had answered mildly: "Sorry, I didn't know it was for me" now worked like everyone else, only a great deal harder.

One old man particularly had Cheshire's sympathy. He needed a lot of attention at night but he came from a quaint old village where such modern innovations as bell pushers which rang a bell fifty yards away were unheard of. Or, if he had ever heard of them, this old man certainly did not understand them. The only sort of bell he understood was one you held firmly in your own hand and shook!

At night, therefore, since he could not be persuaded that by pressing a button someone in the bottom of the building would know that he, at the top, needed attention, he was given a hand bell. This he rang lustily whenever the need arose, and Cheshire was then supposed to awaken and hurry to him.

Unfortunately, however, it was not Cheshire who was woken by these nocturnal clangings. Everyone in Le Court was awakened but not Cheshire. Therefore, he took to sleeping next door to the old man, his bed among the T.B. patients. But still he slept through it all. Also, complained the T.B.s, he snored! So eventually he laid his bed on the floor outside the man's door so that the patient had only to shout and help would be there, whilst the rest of the Home slept on in peace.

Eventually, however, responsibility, the constant demands on his charm and good temper, the work, the long hours and the endless attention needed for the very sick took their toll on his health. By early 1951 it was decided that he must, for a while at least, live a more regular life in a less tiring job.

Cheshire accepted the verdict calmly but with sadness. It meant that he must hand over the administration of his cherished Home, every detail of which bore the imprint of his own personality, to a board of trustees: and no matter how sympathetic or efficient they may be, that is not the same thing as running it oneself.

"You can't scavenge and scrounge with a board of trustees," he sums it up rather sadly, and there is no doubt that he missed the scavenging and scrounging.

Thus, secure in the knowledge that Le Court would be well cared for, he took a new job. He entered Vickers-Armstrongs, on the research side, and returned to work with, of all people, Barnes Wallis of the earthquake bomb.

He moved down to Cornwall to take up his duties at Helston and thenceforth his only connection with Le Court became a place on the committee of trustees and the indestructible aura of his own personality. Technically, though, the Home passed out of his hands.

Chapter Fifteen

TUBERCULOSIS

IT WAS AT the beginning of 1951 that the national Press first got word that Constance Binney was divorcing Cheshire for desertion. Upon being interviewed, Cheshire at once replied:

"Yes. I've entered a formal legal appearance admitting the charge that I deserted her in America five years ago."

In actual fact what had happened was that Constance Binney had become homesick for the States and returned there in 1944. She had endeavoured to persuade her husband to rejoin her after he left Washington, when, in that same year, he had so briefly been on the Military Mission. He, far from being tired of England and by now firmly convinced that the British way of life was better than almost any other, refused.

Quietly, and without rancour, the marriage died.

"In many ways it made things tidier," Cheshire comments. "You see, the position needed clearing up—the legal position, that is. I'm a Roman Catholic now: she was divorced when I married her and the Catholic Church doesn't recognize divorce. Therefore, it couldn't recognize our marriage. In the eyes of my Church it was null and void and I couldn't ever go back to her. It's much better now that we both know where we stand."

✷   ✷   ✷

Cheshire left his work at Le Court because his friends, his family and his priest had all insisted that it was necessary to his mental and physical well-being that he should. Nevertheless, the break was a painful one. His old war-time chief, Sir Ralph Cochrane, now secured him his position at Vickers-Armstrongs.

This post Cheshire accepted with some conviction. He had long since decided that unless a miracle occurred, and to him no miracle seemed probable, there would be a third world war, precipitated by Russia.

He recognized clearly the duty of the British Government to do all in its power to prepare a defence against this aggression, the defence of its citizens. He recognized equally clearly his own duty to contribute his not inconsiderable knowledge and experience of warfare to that preparation. So now he undertook the task of munitions research with as much ardour as previously he had helped his fellow men at Le Court. It was still helping them, he considered: there was a difference in degree, that was all.

As far as he personally was concerned, the job offered every advantage. He had his own Spitfire in which to fly around the country: he had a great deal of freedom of movement, and he lived in a cottage on the Lizard peninsula.

Nevertheless, as a research expert, Cheshire was not particularly happy. The job did not seem to him to be constructive enough, rather the opposite, since the stress was always on the applicability of his work to counter-attack in the event of war. Also he missed the personal contacts and the spiritual warmth of looking after others. It was inevitable that, sooner or later, he would revolt. His heart was still with the sick and the down-and-outs.

The first signal of this revolt came when a young man wrote to him saying that he was an ex-Frogman and an epileptic. Because of his physical disability he had been unable to get a job, had been thrown out of his digs and could find no substitute for either. Immediately Cheshire wrote him to come and live with him in his own cottage at Tredannack.

Almost at the same time he was circling the aerodrome one day when he noticed a cluster of derelict buildings near his home. Immediately his brain seethed with the perfect solution for all his problems.

He, personally, wanted to run homes for the sick. Everyone else told him he needed a regular job with regular hours. All right, he would please both parties. He would have his regular job *and*, if they were available, he would take over these disused buildings and start another home. Promptly he made enquiries.

The buildings, he was told by an officer who regarded him with deep and justifiable suspicion, were deserted, useless and requisitioned. There was no chance whatsoever of getting permission to use them. He inspected them, found that everything derogatory ever said about them was only too palpably true, and set about acquiring them forthwith. Air Ministry, helpful to him as ever, eventually granted him a monthly tenancy. At once he set about repairing the huts.

"Shocking state they were in," he says. "Cows everywhere. Bleak, windswept, no drains, no water or electricity, nothing worked, bog everywhere." Cheshire was about to found his second home. He called it St. Teresa's.

Although a sick man already, he thenceforward devoted all his spare time and energy to the restoration of this group of disused and deserted huts. He and the epileptic ex-Frogman knocked partitions down, painted walls, dug drains and laid bricks.

It was this latter function which Cheshire performed so badly that a local Cornishman could stand it no longer and himself took over. That started a flood of voluntary labour from workmen at Vickers; from men and women on the peninsula; from H.M.S. *Seahawk*, whose personnel spent their leisure building a little chapel for him at St. Teresa's.

"Well, that's very kind of you," remarked Cheshire, using a phrase that was now required of him ten times a day, so violently did people feel it necessary to do things for him. "What can you do?"

"Anything you like," they assured him. He put them promptly on to mending some stoves, all of which seemed somehow, to his inexpert eye, to have become sadly and irretrievably divorced from their flues. Three Petty Officers easily married the disjoined portions of the stoves: and St. Teresa's then showed possibilities of becoming habitable.

Thenceforth, at week-ends and on "Make and Mend" days, there was a steady stream of officers and men from Helston to help Cheshire. Jolly Jack, who will grumble himself to death at the prospect of doing any of the legitimate tasks for which he enlisted, now cheerfully worked like a navvy in his spare time at St. Teresa's.

But still there was no water, no electricity and no drains.

"Never mind," said Cheshire firmly, "the best thing is not to worry. Let's get some patients in!"

Obviously, with patients arriving, the first thing that *had* to be installed was some form of drainage and a septic tank. Spotting an old tank that lay around, apparently needed by nobody, Cheshire promptly decided to steal it.

"It was only a very small one," he explained, thereby hoping to absolve himself. "Couldn't have been more than four hundred gallons." And then, forgetting completely that he was defending himself against a charge of petty larceny, if a four-hundred-gallon tank qualifies as petty larceny, he added unrepentantly: "Better than nothing, anyway." The local Clerk of Works fortunately heard of his need and saved him the crime of theft by giving him the tank and organizing its transport as well.

Having acquired it, Cheshire had then, alone, set about sinking it in the bog.

He knew nothing about drainage and even less about sinking tanks. He was enthusiastic, though; and the delightful thought of patients soon to be cared for, endless hours of extra work and the ease with which he had circumvented the well-intentioned desire of his friends to wean him away from nursing; all this spurred him on.

Six inches down he struck rock. Undeterred, he fetched a sledge hammer and wedges and belted away at the offending obstruction. At which a farmer in the distance, who knew nothing of the rock but observed only a madman slogging at the bog with a sledge hammer, remarked:

"There, m'dear, is a good man gone wrong."

"Eventually," Cheshire continued, "after a terrible sweat, I got the tank in. Three hours later I came out to find its top not level with the ground but five feet above it. The hole I'd dug had filled with water and the tank was floating."

It was not long, however, with his first patients already in residence, before Cheshire decided that this first tank was wholly inadequate. As usually happens when Cheshire decides that he needs something, it turned up. Some way down the road he observed another and much bigger and equally disused tank.

"Whose is that?" he asked the locals. They said they thought it was nobody's.

"Well, then," argued Cheshire, with irresistible logic, "in that case no one would object if I took it, would they?" So he took it, and no one objected, least of all the locals who were accustomed to him now and would really not have noticed if he had gone into Helston and removed the Town Hall. He planned to sink his new tank in the ground near the huts. Once it was in, he felt confident he could somehow induce the local authorities to empty it whenever it became full. Typical

Cheshire technique! The authorities thereupon, unprompted, offered to empty it twice a week. Typical Cheshire success!!

The hole to accommodate this monstrous tank, however, needed to be 40 × 8 × 7 feet, in waterlogged clay. No one at all cared for the idea of trying to dig such a hole by hand.

"Specially," Cheshire comments, "after my experience with the *first* tank."

In consequence they did not dig the hole for it by hand. They prevailed upon an official excavator with a magnificent machine which happened to be passing their way, to do it for them quite unofficially.

Whilst the hole was being dug the Petty Officers were waterproofing the tank. "Terrible job," Cheshire says. "All sorts of joints and things. I didn't understand it at all; but they did, so that was all right." Then they managed to "persuade" a naval crane-driver to whip his giant crane off the road for a minute or two, collect the tank, bring it up and lower it into the newly dug hole. Finally, they dumped about "ten tons of rock", Cheshire's own carefree estimate, on top of the tank and made sure that it did not float. St. Teresa's now had drainage.

The only hitch in the whole masterly operation was that when the naval crane, so illicitly helping them, came to leave the scene of their triumph, they found, to their horror, that it was bogged and it was needed next day at Culdrose when flying duties would be resumed on the Naval Air Station.

"We were in a proper pickle then," Cheshire said. "Fortunately, though, one of the patients who had just arrived was a very experienced navvy. He had a glorious time directing us all from his window as to how to unbog this wretched crane. He must've known something about it, though, because the next morning we got it out."

Improvisation was usually the order of the day, and there

were makeshifts which would have delighted Heath Robinson. At one time there was so little furniture that string was stretched across the end of the beds so that patients might hang up their clothes.

So St. Teresa's started, grew and flourished. It now has seventeen patients, all chronically sick, and a long waiting-list. Plans are afoot to rehouse the patients in a larger building in Penzance.

*   *   *

At Christmas-time 1951, Cheshire received a letter from a woman who asked him most urgently to take in her son. He was an ex-Bomber Command man with a D.F.C., but he was now mental and she could no longer manage him, whilst he, on his side, refused to leave her to go to a hospital. To Cheshire, she felt, he might go. To Cheshire he did.

But once Cheshire had received him into St. Teresa's he quickly realized that either the man must be sent away again, because of the effect he had on other patients, *or* a new home must be started specially for neurosis cases. Characteristically Cheshire chose the latter course. He set up a new home, close to St. Teresa's, and called it *Holy Cross*. This now has several ex-service patients and awaits only the extension of its buildings and the help of more staff before it accepts others.

So, briskly as ever, scrounging, improvising, cheering and working in his time off from Vickers, Cheshire now continued the task he had been persuaded so sensibly to lay down at Le Court. The same voluntary labour helped: the same official support arrived: the same welfare and charitable organizations found the lure of the Cheshire technique too much for them and generously did their bit. The most important thing was that all the patients were happy. 1951 passed and the new year arrived.

He now found himself wearying suddenly. He was weary of Vickers-Armstrongs, whose work he felt he should never have

undertaken: he was weary in himself because he never seemed
to be well. Every second week, it seemed, he went down with
influenza.

"It was a standing joke at Vickers, my 'flu," he said. "I was
getting fed up with it. I felt such a fool."

So he resigned from Vickers-Armstrongs and, for a few
happy weeks, devoted himself solely to the building up of St.
Teresa's and Holy Cross.

In spite of his active work a visiting priest took him aside
and, with remarkably prophetic insight, told him that his rôle
was not to do work himself but to influence others.

"The success of your plans will always depend upon how
much you manage to work through other people," the priest
asserted. Cheshire was not greatly impressed. He belonged to
the "do it yourself" school.

A fortnight later, out of the blue, the Press phoned him in
Cornwall.

"Is it true that you are leaving Cornwall to take up new
work?" they asked.

Emphatically, indignantly almost, Cheshire denied it.

Then, the very next morning, without warning, he collapsed. A thorough examination revealed that he suffered from
severe tuberculosis of one lung and that further work was
quite impossible. He was rushed off to St. Michael's Hospital
and there, it seemed, Cheshire's work must cease. In spite of
his indignant denial to the Press he had moved from Cornwall,
he was about to take up new projects, and he was to work
through others. "My life has always been full of surprises,"
he sums it all up contentedly.

About a year before this time the old Le Court building at
Liss had begun to crumble. Cheshire himself has a spirited,
carefree description of what happened.

"There was an underground stream running beneath it,"
he says light-heartedly. "No one seemed to know anything

about it until the whole building collapsed." Only the wild twinkle in his eye and the wide smile on his face told you that here was another typical flight of Cheshire extravagance and exaggeration.

"Everyone got in a terrible state and kept asking 'what are we going to do?' Don't blame them really. We needed £30,000 to save the place" he confessed. "Anyway, I said 'buy five pounds' worth of bricks and start laying them.'" His eyes flashed with retrospective regret as he remembered how helpless he had been to lay them himself and realized that now there was little practical help he could render either to Le Court or to St. Teresa's.

"Once you show you're ready to have a go yourself," he maintained, "others will join you." Ever since 1939 others have been joining Cheshire. And whenever they do so he smiles charmingly at them, says "That's very kind of you", and back they come for more!

The trustees disapproved violently of Cheshire's frivolous anecdote about the collapse of Le Court. They told the story much more accurately. Yet, in the unforced gaiety and inaccuracy of Cheshire's tale there is a winning, healthy confidence in the future which is naturally lacking in the justifiable anxieties expressed by his trustees. Cheshire believes and knows that where public support is necessary for his Homes it will come. His trustees work hard and practically to ensure that it will. There is an equal amount to be said in support of either point of view, and, each being complementary to the other, both are necessary.

And yet circumstances do seem to have proved Cheshire's blind, tranquil faith to be more than justified. Le Court and its threatened disintegration is a case in point. For no sooner did the old house become imperilled than the · Carnegie United Kingdom Trust stepped into the breach. They did so, however, because they had complete confidence in his trustees.

Again both parties seem justified. In their annual report the Carnegie Trust stated:

"Towards the end of 1951, our attention was drawn to an experiment in social work which had been started, on his own initiative and out of his own resources, by Group Captain Leonard Cheshire, V.C., one of the most distinguished bomber pilots of the last war. A chain of circumstances, which are part of his personal history and need not be recounted here, had led him to the conclusion that there was a real need to make some sort of provision, on a communal basis, for people who were infirm of body, through physical disablement or for some other reasons, but did not require constant or even frequent medical attention and ought not to be permanent inmates of hospital wards, even if beds could be provided for them. He had acquired an old mansion called Le Court, near Liss, Hampshire, and there had collected a small community of disabled people, young and old and of both sexes, who lived together as a family and did what they could both to help one another and to lend a hand in the general running of the home.

"When it first came to our notice, the Cheshire Foundation Home for the Sick, as it is now called, was just able to meet its running costs, largely with the help of voluntary contributions from outside, but the house was an old-fashioned one, ill-equipped for institutional purposes and sadly in need of alteration and improvement. Medical and health services have always been regarded as lying outside the scope of the Trust, but the social aspect of this particular venture so appealed to us that we were ready to consider a capital grant for reconstruction. When, however, we got detailed reports on the building, it was clear that, at the best, only a patchwork job could be made of the existing premises, and it seemed wiser to enlarge our ideas and provide funds for the erection of a completely new home, specially designed for its purpose,

which might serve as a model for similar enterprises else-
where. Suitable plans have been prepared, and we have
agreed, in principle, to meet the building cost, which has
been estimated, in round figures, at between £60,000 and
£65,000."

Swiftly the requisite building licences were obtained and
plans drawn up. And on June 20th, 1953, almost eight years
after Nagasaki, the foundation stone of a building that is
now complete was laid by Marshal of the Royal Air Force
Lord Tedder. So Le Court, in spite of underground streams
and Cheshire's lurid account of its total disintegration, still
flourishes.

The Carnegie United Kingdom Trust's function, however,
is not to foster medical projects. Social work is its aim. For
that reason, therefore, although they rebuilt Le Court, they
could not equip it. Nor could they endow or sustain it for the
future. The task of raising funds to attain these medical ends
has fallen on the trustees of Le Court and upon Cheshire
himself. Neither the trustees, with their business-like hard
work, nor Cheshire, with his sublime faith, have ever allowed
the Home to want for anything.

Now that he was so ill, the trustees took over St.
Teresa's as well as Le Court.

Under their administration Le Court became a Home not
just for anyone who knocked on the door but for the young
chronic-sick suffering from various forms of paralysis. They
mention casually such diseases as disseminated sclerosis,
muscular atrophy and spondylitis. But to young men and
women suffering from them, becoming daily more physically
handicapped by them and doomed to lifelong inactivity in
sterile hospital wards because of them, Le Court suddenly
offered what had never been possible before—the combination
of medical treatment, a home of their own and the possibility
of helping in the running and maintenance of that home.

Here was no soul-destroying charity; no impersonal, impatient public-hospitalization; no impotent lying in bed and contributing nothing. The proper environment which no National Health Scheme could envisage, or afford if it had envisaged it, was now made available at Le Court. Thirty-four patients there today and a long waiting-list for the future are evidence of its value.

Needless to say, in spite of small payments by patients and subsidies from various official bodies, expenses are heavy. Running costs in 1952 were about £13,000, and of that £3,500 had to be raised from voluntary sources. And that was for Le Court only. Now there is St. Teresa's, Holy Cross and a new Home at Bromley known as St. Cecilia's.

Nevertheless, Homes such as these, popularly known as the "Cheshire Homes", have assumed the magnificent rôle of providing a full life and the proper treatment for patients to whom existence would otherwise be intolerable. Also taking Le Court as an example, out of the total amount of £13,000 they ask only one quarter from voluntary contributions, which does not impose at all harshly upon public generosity.

With unerring instinct, the public has also sensed that this is so. At Le Court very considerable help arrives each Sunday from Portsmouth and local Toc H groups. Entertainment is provided by other bodies. Student organizations and Oxford undergraduates lend aid with the customary violent enthusiasm of youthful ardour and the scholar momentarily released from his books.

At St. Teresa's, where the patients are slightly more incapacitated even than those at Le Court, the story is the same. The Cornishmen are most sympathetic. Furthermore the Navy, as they have from the very beginning, send constant help from their station at Culdrose, near Helston.

And all the time, surrounded by this bustle of administration, medical treatment and outside support, the patients themselves run their own lives with energy and success. They have a Welfare Fund, a committee to run it and a constitution to guide the committee. Petrol for outings, stock for their canteen, radio sets, cinema tickets, Christmas tit-bits; all these aspects of their domestic life are their own responsibility. The Welfare Fund is their own personal stake, and a substantial one, in the running of the Home which they have made their home.

*   *   *

Whilst all this rearrangement of control and delegation of power went on, Cheshire himself lay in St. Michael's Hospital. Here he evolved his own special technique for being ill. It consisted of furious mental activity, which more than compensated for his physical inertia and a steady stream of cheerful and disrespectful backchat to all the staff who tried to treat him firmly.

He insisted, with hoots of laughter, that he was bullied, ill-treated, underfed and anything else that occurred to his outrageous imagination. The days passed amiably and no one would have suspected that the man who joked about everything, who spoke with such unforced charm and gaiety and whose smile was the most cheerful thing to have happened to them since that unforgettable summer of 1949, was in fact tuberculous.

It was soon decided, however, that his condition was so serious that he must move to another sanatorium. It was to be the King Edward VII Sanatorium at Midhurst, a Royal institution, and he was to come under the hands of Sir Geoffrey Todd, an Australian specialist with a world-wide reputation.

Shortly before he was due to depart a Sister came to see him, Sister Theophila.

"Sister Theophila," Cheshire explains, "is a very strong woman. Very strong character. Difficult to resist when she's made her mind up." And Sister Theophila had made up her mind.

"Leonard," she said firmly, "what clothes have you got? You're going from here to the Midhurst Sanatorium and you've got to go properly dressed."

It so happened that Cheshire had no clothes at all to speak of, and was perfectly happy to go to Midhurst, or to Speakers' Corner for that matter, in his pyjamas.

"I'm all right, thank you, Sister," he replied evasively. "Got plenty in my bag."

"Where's your bag? Let me look."

"Well, it's under the bed, as a matter of fact. Covered in rubbish. Too much trouble for you to get it out . . ." But Sister Theophila had already got it out and opened it.

"You have nothing," she accused him icily.

"No, Sister," he replied, feeling quite nine years old.

"Well," she declared, "you're not going to Midhurst dressed so that you'll disgrace us. I'll see to it myself." And see to it she did. Cheshire found himself most respectably clothed when he entered the new sanatorium: and in addition, in his bag, he carried a magnificent Jaeger bed-jacket specially tailored for him and produced in record time at the behest of the irresistible Sister Theophila herself.

So began his two-year stay at the King Edward VII Sanatorium, during which he was to undergo four operations on his chest, to be cured of tuberculosis but to fight a severe battle against infection suffered in the deep wounds of the incisions themselves. These were the circumstances that were to be the background to the most productive period of his life.

Chapter Sixteen

A VISIT TO CHESHIRE

IT IS NOW TIME for you to meet Cheshire personally and
as he is today. One learns that he was Britain's youngest
Group Captain in 1943, that he has three D.S.O.s,
the D.F.C. and the Victoria Cross, and immediately he
becomes an unreal figure of great glamour and quite un-
approachable distinction. One knocks on his door in the
hospital and experiences a sense of acute apprehension and
excitement. What will this extraordinary and legendary man
look like?

"Come in," a precise voice instructs firmly. One enters;
and there he is.

An oval face, with a strong chin and a slightly pursed
mouth, looks upwards, politely, agreeably and with intense
reserve. Heavy eyebrows meet confusedly over his nose,
brown eyes peer at one with a second's intense penetration,
then soften into blandness. His haircut is quite terrible and his
handshake uncompromisingly firm. He looks neither ill nor
extraordinary. It is very disconcerting.

"Nice of you to come," he says and smiles, a brief, en-
chanting smile that crinkles his eyes and lights his whole
face and reveals perfect teeth. Then the smile has gone and
gravely he indicates a chair.

"Have a seat." One looks at the chair. It is already occupied
with a nickel-plated gadget. When this is held up to him
enquiringly he says: "Hair dryer. Put it somewhere. Floor,

I suppose," so the hair dryer goes on to the floor and one sits down, acutely conscious of the fact that, in the brief second of his first, shrewd scrutiny, Cheshire has learnt all about oneself, but about Cheshire one still knows nothing whatsoever.

The room is a splendid chaos of books, pieces of paper, cardboard folders and tape-recorder. Also it is icy cold. This temperature, which would kill a person in normal health, is apparently quite innocuous and beneficial to T.B. patients, and Cheshire himself appears not even to notice it. However, his courtesy is unfailing and he at once observes that his guest is quietly refrigerating in the chair from which he so recently evicted a hair dryer.

"Shut the window if you feel the cold," he suggests agreeably. And round the corner of his lips there is the faintest suspicion of a smile, a smile compounded equally of hospitality and benevolent malice!

Then he lies back, reserved, reticent, completely in command of the situation, his chin resting on the joined fingertips of both hands, and waits to see why you have come. Whilst he waits he watches you with an oblique glance out of the corner of his eye. It is a three-cornered glance; behind it his mind is obviously not entirely with you. He has so many visitors and they almost all say and ask the same things. And Cheshire is a very busy man.

He is a surprise. He doesn't at all resemble the glamorous warrior one had expected. He looks rather ordinary, in fact; and his high forehead would sit more naturally on the face of an Oxford don than on that of a hero of World War II. Only the unmistakable note of authority in every syllable of his crisp voice gives any indication of the man who, at twenty-five, became a much decorated Group Captain.

The oblique glance and the silence persist. Nervously one fumbles for cigarettes, and then remembers that the man in bed is tuberculous and perhaps smoking will make him cough.

"May I smoke?"

"Yes, do. Fire ahead," he murmurs, in tones of such superb disinterest that one knows instantly that had one asked ' may I go jump in the lake?" the answer would have been exactly the same.

"There are some cigarettes on the dressing-table," he offers and then remembers, as one politely accepts his offer and restores one's own cigarettes, that the packet is empty and he has no matches anyway. At this, in a situation that should be embarrassing to himself, he suddenly hoots with laughter and all tension vanishes. He looks like a mischievous small boy and exudes friendliness.

As he laughs and you relax you notice that his eyes aren't brown after all; they are hazel. His teeth are not quite perfect, as you had thought, but a little bent in front. You realize that he is elusive and difficult of description. You define him at your own peril.

"Now, what can I do for you?" he asks. Provided one tells him at once, not at any time reverting to small-talk, the oblique glance changes into a square look of frank interest and the conversation runs smoothly, punctuated only by those schoolboy hoots of Cheshire mirth. He talks well and precisely, with unfailing cheerfulness, enjoying most a story against himself, and only retiring into that eyes-almost-averted, polite silence when the topic becomes trivial or the questions vague or tentative.

Ask him the bluntest, most personal or technical question and he will reply at once with lively candour and no inhibitions at all. But feel your way cannily towards a subject, and he will immediately sense what it is you want to know, but have not asked, and become impeccably polite but maddeningly vague on that and all other subjects.

I remember asking him, without the faintest attempt at courtesy, why he became a Roman Catholic. He accepted the question with not a flicker of surprise or displeasure, even though he knew that I was not a Catholic myself, indeed not anything in particular of any religion. Briefly and objectively, he related the sequence of events; the conversation about God in a Mayfair bar; a B29 floating serenely above the doomed city beneath it; the death of a homeless man in a quiet room at Le Court.

I remember asking why he married Constance Binney only to desert her four years later. Again, and without hesitation, he answered frankly.

To the question, should his marriage be discussed in this book, he replied: "Well, of course. It's the truth; it happened, didn't it?"

To the question: "Wnat was the supreme moment of the war for you, speaking personally?" he answered, with swift emphasis: "Munich."

But when, in my earliest, fumbling moments of interview, I had enquired: "How do you keep your nails in such good order?" he only responded "Cut them when they get too long" . . . and his eyes slid away from mine, his mind going with them, so that it took quite ten minutes of hard talking to regain his attention.

After a visitor has been with him a short time Cheshire organizes some tea. This is brought in on a tray and, as the nurse puts it down, he says:

"Thank you, Crasher," and smiles that special smile that has always endeared him to ground crew, volunteer workers and nursing staff. "She used to drop things," he explains when the nickname startles his guest.

He indulges in an incessant and engaging banter with all the staff who enter his room.

"Matron won't be pleased when she sees how you've left me," he threatens, pointing at his own mess of papers and cardboard boxes; and, "she's the most troublesome of the lot," as he introduces another nurse.

At another walking patient, a squadron leader called Preddy, he directed a steady stream of goading insults about Australians.

"Don't know why you always abuse the Aussies whenever I come here," Preddy complained.

"You're an Australian, aren't you?" Cheshire demanded.

"No, South African," the other denied.

"Well," exploded Cheshire, "you've been wasting my time!"

Nothing and no one, it seems, can quite subdue in him this tendency towards frivolity. For example, one day as he lay in bed, surrounded by the usual chaos of letters, files, tape-recorder and notes, the door opened and Queen Elizabeth the Queen Mother entered. She was visiting the hospital and had asked, unexpectedly, to see Cheshire, the man whom her husband had decorated so often.

Casting one appalled glance at the litter all over his bed, Cheshire decided that nothing, short of dragging it under the blankets with him, could be done about it. He felt a swift spasm of profound relief that at least he was wearing Sister Theophila's smart Jaeger bed-jacket. His bed might look frightful, indeed he could see from the Matron's expression that it did, but he, at any rate, looked rather smart.

With her usual delightful smile and easy manner the Queen Mother asked him how he was. With an equally delightful smile and his own usual mischievousness Cheshire replied: "I'm very well thank you, Ma'am, except that I'm shockingly bullied by the sisters."

As the nurses at the open doorway gave every indication of swooning utterly away the Queen Mother leant forward and murmured: "Yes I know: I know what it's like." Her mischievousness was just as apparent as his own. The staff hurriedly unswooned with relief and after a gracious farewell the Queen Mother left to continue her inspection of the rest of the Royal sanatorium and her visits to other privileged patients.

When other patients in the sanatorium undergo the same operation as he himself has endured, four times now, he sends them a cheerful note of encouragement on the night before.

Nor is his correspondence limited only to the inhabitants of the stately sanatorium. Every day, in his beautifully neat and wellnigh-indecipherable handwriting, he sends out a wad of letters to his friends and helpers. And, as well as that, he dictates on to his tape-recorder another swathe of letters which, when she receives the tape that he has posted her, an ex-W.A.A.F. types out in her own limited spare time and then posts back to him for his signature.

For this invaluable but onerous task she receives no more than his warm smile when she visits him and the invariable good-natured banter that he keeps for his special friends. As with everyone else, that, to her, seems to be enough.

He has a tube draining the infection in his lung to which he refers contemptuously as "this thing in my chest", and for more than eighteen months he has been fighting off his disability.

Yet he lies there in his bed, eyes gleaming with the joy of living, diving into odd cardboard boxes, his "filing system", for papers concerning his various plans, dictating letters and speeches on to his tape recorder, studying theology, back-chatting with all and sundry, organizing those who suddenly feel impelled to offer their services, serenely contemplating his new-found faith and apparently finding his existence wholly satisfactory.

It would be difficult, in this our present age of ghastly Peace, to find a more tranquil and genuinely peaceful man than Leonard Cheshire, V.C., who, in 1952, was stricken down with a disease from which he is still not fully recovered. But merely to be tranquil and peaceful is not, for him, enough. A bell rings in the corridor. Crasher appears looking polite but firm. Visiting hours are over.

As you leave, he smiles again, but already his mind is vanishing from you on to other things.

"Thank you for coming down," he says. "I hope you'll come again."

You say good-bye.

"Drive back carefully," he advises, a trifle absently; and, as you close the door, you wonder whether his mind as he said the words has returned to the riotous days of his Alfa Romeo at Oxford, or to the accident he had outside York with Willie Tait, or whether he has just said the first agreeable thing that came into his head. You don't know. That is the enigma of Leonard Cheshire's personality.

Chapter Seventeen

BEDSIDE CRUSADE

N o s o o n e r d i d Cheshire find himself chained to a bed and popularly supposed to be unable to work any longer than, as related, he obtained a tape recorder and proceeded briskly to dictate letters on to it.

Far from being *hors de combat,* as people had concluded, he was maintaining a close contact with the outside world and channelling much of its interest into the improbable reservoir of his own hospital room. From there he redirected it with precision and authority to irrigate his schemes as he himself thought best.

He appreciated that, having handed over all his Homes to two boards of trustees, he must no longer interfere. Therefore, if he were to work, which he thoroughly intended doing, he must work in entirely fresh fields. For a while, apart from keeping in touch with people and steadily increasing his sphere of outside contacts, he could not quite see how to do it.

Four factors helped him to decide. The first was a book: the second a disused bus, ugly but perfect for his purpose: the third a stranger who offered to help in any way at all but looked like himself being disused because there was no job available for him: and the fourth a disused idea. It happened like this.

Paul Brickhill's war book, *The Dam Busters*, dealt with the history of 617 Squadron right through the days of its training under Gibson, its dam raids, its training under

Cheshire, its rocket-site raids and through to the end of the war. It mentioned many distinguished pilots but, as the only surviving V.C. and one of the squadron's four successive leaders, Cheshire inevitably received far more fan mail than any of the others. One of these letters came from a small boy asking for his autograph, a very common request.

Cheshire replied from the sanatorium in a personal letter, a typical Cheshire touch. The small boy then wrote saying that he was sorry the Group Captain was ill and he wished he could give him some of his mother's raspberries. Gravely Cheshire replied again and thanked him.

Not long afterwards boy and parents, on their way for a holiday, called in to deliver him some of mother's raspberries. Before they departed, father, hardly aware of what he was saying, had offered any help he could give. He was not a Catholic: he was not even convinced that Cheshire's plans stood any great chance of success, but he did feel that he should lend a hand.

Cheshire smiled at him, said: "That's very kind of you," and, as they left him, lay back on his bed wondering just how he could use this offer of help.

Meanwhile, a fellow-patient (an ex-Marston Moor pilot) who owned a fleet of buses, had remarked that two of them were no use to him; they were different from the others and, as the ugly ducklings of the brood, he wanted to get rid of them. Cheshire, who didn't care what difference there was between these buses and any other buses, so long as they were disused buses, promptly acquired them.

Now he had both a bus and an offer of help which he had not yet called upon. He also had his disused idea.

Three weeks before he had fallen ill, Cheshire had decided to tour the country preaching a simple and practical Christianity. Tuberculosis knocked that on the head.

For nine months in St. Michael's he lay, as he says, "like a

log," turning over ideas and being gently nursed by the good
nuns who were the hospital's staff. Then he conceived the
idea of a bus that preached without him, by the medium of his
voice reproduced from the tape-recorder that lay by his bed.

But he had no bus as yet, and, even if he had, there was no
one to run it. Then, when he entered the sanatorium and the
night before he acquired his buses, two friends arrived in
Britain from Hong Kong.

Rupert and Patty Mace had been prisoners of the Japanese
during the war. They offered to help Cheshire in any way
possible. Promptly he asked them to "organize" the bus.
This they did, but the one thing above all that they lacked was
a driver. They lacked it because Rupert had only one leg,
having lost the other under the tender ministrations of his
Japanese war-time hosts, and could not drive himself.

Thus, at this moment, Cheshire found himself with an idea,
a bus and the small boy's father who offered to do anything
he could; three factors which quickly added up to a whole in
Cheshire's fertile mind.

The obvious thing to do was to combine the three. He
decided to ask his volunteer to drive the bus and to use the
bus itself, equipped by the Maces, as a travelling testament to
Britain's ancient and traditional faith of Christianity.

This faith, Cheshire pointed out, had made Britain the nation
she is. Nowadays, he said, the world needed Britain more than
ever before. Britain therefore, if she were to help the world,
needed the faith. And the faith, if it were to flourish, needed the
people.

Therefore, to attract people to Christianity, he would
equip the bus with a crib in which a tableau-display would
attract attention and then, to the onlookers who gathered
round, he would himself talk, through the medium of his tape-
recorder.

"We had two lambs in the crib for Christmas. Everyone's

mad about lambs." Later he had fantail pigeons: and, of course, the British are traditionally fanatical about pigeons, so that was a success too.

The volunteer worker drove the bus round to various pitches in London, plugged in the tape-machine to the power of agreeably-disposed cafés and restaurants, and in no time at all a crowd was gathering round. Soon music was heard from the inside of the bus, then the smooth, precise accents of Leonard Cheshire. Chained to a hospital bed he may have been: but he addressed thousands of Londoners nevertheless.

"At first," he admits, "people are a bit cautious about coming inside the bus to look at the crib. Think they'll be caught for something. Then we tell them it's free and they start to climb in; obviously, though, still wondering what the catch is!"

So the thing grew. He decided that a travelling bus in Cornwall would be a good idea. Then, in a characteristic outburst of Cheshirian enthusiasm and fantasy, he demanded: "Why shouldn't I have *thousands* of buses and send them all over the country?" The reasons, both financial and administrative, why he shouldn't have thousands of buses travelling all over the country are only too obvious. Someone firmly told him why and the elaborate fantasy then died.

But the *two* buses he did own flourished. Exerting that effortless though, one suspects, deliberate magnetism of his over his visitors and chance acquaintances, he was never short of helpers to run them. A W.R.A.C. major, Shelagh Howe, long a devoted supporter, a Mrs. Platt, and the man who drove for him have been the backbone of the project outside the hospital.

Inside, men like Squadron Leader Leonard Preddy and a determined little Scot called Jock Alston have attended to much of the detail of the tableau-displays themselves. Yet Preddy is a non-Catholic and Alston is not only non-Catholic but, along with Cheshire, shares the painful honour of being the sanatorium's oldest inhabitant. That one man of another faith and a second of ill-health equal to Cheshire's own should both work so enthusiastically is indicative of the degree to which Cheshire can indeed "get people to do things for him."

The idea of sending a bus to Cornwall sprang quite naturally to Cheshire's mind because of his association, through St. Teresa's and Holy Cross, with that county, and as a gesture of reciprocation for all the kindness the Cornishmen had shown him. They have always had a soft spot in his heart.

He had already gone out of his way to repay their kindness once by having sent to him from Spain a beautiful reproduction of the Macerena of Seville which he forwarded to some Catholic fishermen: now he would offer them the services of his second bus.

So the idea started and grew and became firmly established. Now he has three buses—and though it is unlikely in the extreme that he will ever acquire the 997 others he once so blithely mentioned, it is also beyond doubt, unless he himself should so wish it, that any he should acquire will never cease to function.

*   *   *

Running the buses, though, was not without its troubles, especially in the West End of London.

There the pitches they chose also happened to be the pitches of another profession entirely, indeed the oldest in the world! So the Cheshire bus, its back half a gambolling of lambs or a fluttering of pigeons, would pull up in a street that was a parading ground of "the girls."

It was a form of competition which had the girls frankly nonplussed. Drunks, the Law, curious sightseers—all these they could cope with. But a bus full of pigeons, carrying a large photograph of a slim, handsome V.C., pouring out a pleasantly modulated murmur of light classical music interspersed with the Christian doctrine, that was altogether beyond them.

Wisely, then, they compromised, gave the project their good will, stood around, somewhat incongruously, one must admit, and listened: and then, when they had heard the programme right through, went briskly back to work.

However, there could, in such a set-up, be crises. One of these befell Shelagh Howe.

Observing a man who watched and dithered and could make up his mind neither to approach the bus and find out for himself nor to go away and forget about it, Shelagh eventually could stand it no longer and advanced upon him to invite him to enter the bus and look for himself.

Immediately, in a street teeming with prostitutes, she was stopped by a policeman on suspicion of soliciting! It took twenty minutes' solid talking on the part of the man, Shelagh Howe and the girls themselves to extricate her from a situation she herself found at once hilarious and embarrassing.

Mrs. Platt, too, had her awkward moments. A street trader who sold flowers watched them idly. He seemed faintly interested but made no move to enter the bus.

"Come in and have a seat," she invited. Promptly the man gave his answer in a stream of East End oaths which were summed up in his final contemptuous phrase: "If I want to sit anywhere it won't be in any flipping bus, it'll be in the bloody pub!" And off he stormed.

Ten minutes later he was back. "Sorry, lady," he apologized, "I didn't know it was the Group Captain's bus. Would you give him this from me?" Very handsomely he presented her with a small bunch of heather and then, uneasily but bravely, climbed into the bus.

As against these trials and tribulations, though, there are

the nights when crowds gather and the bus workers really
feel that they are making headway. One Easter, for example, in
a single week, 2,000 enquiries were made, 1,000 pamphlets
were distributed and six hundred booklets were sold.

Though the bus tableaux had always been popular they had
never before drawn with such magnetism as this, and they had
never made the impression that this display was making. The
reason for this is simple enough; Cheshire had at last found
the right way of exploiting his idea.

As always when he conceives a plan the problem had been
"how to execute it?" As always when confronted with this
problem he took a step forward in the general direction and
waited for the perfect solution to present itself. Thus he had
acted, too, with his theory about low-marking for bombers,
with Le Court in its dilapidation, with St. Teresa's and its lack
of plumbing. The doves and lambs had been a pleasant
notion. This last display was a striking one and the booklet on
it was deservedly popular.

The booklet was on a subject very dear to Cheshire's
heart, the Shroud of Turin, and he wrote it himself. The
tableau in the bus, in this Easter week, was also devoted to that
much-disputed relic.

Thus Len Preddy, Jock Alston, several other Midhurst
patients, a handful of the hospital staff and Cheshire himself
had all worked to convert the crib of the bus into a vaulted-
tomb.

With blue draping they achieved a shadowy cavern, entered
through a narrow gap two thirds the way up the bus towards
the driver's seat.

The outside wall of this tomb they camouflaged cunningly
as rock wall, and at the foot of this wall grew moss and ferns,
and small boulders sprawled. It was not at all unusual in those
days for Cheshire's visitors to find themselves abruptly, but
with the greatest possible charm, invited by their host to go

out and steal rocks and greenery from the hospital gardens
and bring them surreptitiously to the bus.

Inside the blue-dark depths of the tomb again, at the far
end and in one corner, was a tiny altar adorned only with a
cross and two small candles.

The faint glow of the candles fell steadily and with extra-
ordinary effect upon what appeared to be the shadowy form of
Christ Himself, lying life-size and serene, as He had been in
His tomb before the Resurrection.

The effect was achieved by using the enlargement, blown-
up from inches to a full six feet, of a small photograph of the
Shroud of Turin. And this strip of linen, many people all
over the world now fully believe, itself contains what is in
effect a photograph of Jesus Christ after His burial.

Cheshire is one of those people and here are the facts
he has put together about the Shroud.

It is rather narrower than an ordinary bed sheet and about
twice as long. It must be the most disputed piece of linen
in all the history of the world since cloth was first woven,
because it is alleged to be the winding sheet in which Christ
was wrapped, in the Jewish fashion, after He was taken down
from the cross.

There are gaps in its history and questions implicit in its
very survival which cast doubts on its authenticity. On the
other hand there are arguments so strong in support of its
claims that to dispute them seems madness.

Be that as it may, the Shroud for many centuries remained
in Turin, a holy relic but with no greater significance than that.
Now let Cheshire's own words tell the story:

"On close inspection it showed nothing but a series of
indistinct brownish stains merging one into the other.
From a distance it revealed the shadowy life-size outline of a
man, but with a curious air of unreality, which threw out

even the great engraver Dürer and caused him to represent
the body as deformed. The Christian world, in fact, had long
given up hope of reconstructing the features of Christ,
whose body it was known once to have covered; and with
the passing of the years its public exposition became less
and less frequent.

"Such was the position in 1898 when, after having been
locked away in its silver casket for thirty years, it was once
more exposed for public view. It was then that for the first
time in its history it came under the camera, and in the
obscurity of a dark-room yielded up its secret. As Signor
Pia, the official photographer, watched his first plate developing, he saw appearing, not the brownish stains in reverse
and therefore less decipherable, but the clear imprint of a
human face. For such an extraordinary phenomenon there
could only be one explanation, and it was instantly understood by a photographer. The imprint on the Shroud was
in reverse—a negative. And if this was so, it could be
nothing else than a true and faithful picture of the body it
had once covered. It is said that this devout man all but
fainted as the meaning of what he was gazing at penetrated
his understanding. For at that moment he was the only
living man, indeed the only man for nearly 1,900 years,
who knew exactly what had been the appearance of
Christ.

"The news of what had happened in Pia's dark-room
caused an upheaval in the world of science. It also caused an
upheaval in the world of scholarship. The scientists decided
that there was a real problem which called for investigation
and set about investigating it. The scholars turned against the
Shroud on the slender evidence of a handful of fourteenth-
century documents.

"On April 21st, 1902, there took place at the French
Academy of Science what has been described as the most

dramatic meeting since the day when Pasteur made his report on the vaccine for the cure of rabies. Yves Delage, a biologist of world repute and an unbeliever in religion, pronounced the result of a year and a half's scientific investigation of the photographic evidence, of which the following is a brief summary:

"(1) Both figures are as exact as a negative formed by light on a photographic plate. They are furthermore anatomically flawless. That an artist, even if well versed in the principles of photography and the retouching of negatives, could paint in such a manner seems hardly possible. That he should do so centuries before a negative had ever been heard of and yet succeed in preserving so delicate and marvellous an expression, which is at least equal in beauty to any of the world's masterpieces, is utterly inconceivable.

"(2) The process of painting on fabric at that time involved the deposit of pigment on cloth, thereby partially or completely hiding the thread. Yet under the microscope there is nothing to be seen but a delicate stain absorbed by the fabric with every thread visible and no sign whatsoever of pigment. Thus the artist would have had to use materials and to apply a technique hitherto unknown.

"Delage, however, had not yet come to the end of his findings. Having demonstrated that the Shroud was not the work of any human hand, he went on to prove that it bore a full and exact record of every detail of Christ's suffering and death—so exact and so detailed that it could not possibly have belonged to anyone else. 'It is Christ,' he said, 'who has impressed the figure of Himself on the Shroud. And if it is not Christ, then who is it?—some malefactor executed for his crimes? How reconcile this with the admirable expression of nobility which you see on His countenance?'

"The members of the Academy, who received this report very favourably, would undoubtedly have given it an official vote of approval but for an unexpected development. M. Berthelot, the Academy's permanent secretary who was presiding at the meeting, was what is called a Free Thinker. He had already tried to prevent Delage from reporting his findings to the Academy, but had been over-ruled by the president. He now refused to put the findings to the vote, and as editor of the official Academy minutes refused to publish the proofs put forward by Delage in support of his findings.

"This was a situation which the Press was only too quick to exploit. Anti-religion was the fashion of the time. From different parts of Europe historians were claiming that the Shroud was a fake. Their case was based on the evidence of certain documents stating that a fourteenth-century artist had confessed to forging the image, and against the positive and unanswerable findings of science these were of little, if any, value. But the men who were pressing the attack were Catholics and leading intellectuals—a German professor, a French historian, and an English scholar—and this, added to Berthelot's action, was to prove the decisive factor. When a false rumour spread that the Academy had rejected Delage's report, the Catholic world of scholarship lined up behind the historians. Delage himself was attacked and ridiculed by the Press and the critics. The rest of the world argued that if Catholics themselves did not believe in the Shroud, then there was little point in pursuing the matter any further. And so the Shroud was relegated to another thirty years of retirement and obscurity.

"Yet for all that, the scientists knew what they were doing: they never gave up the investigation.

"It was in 1931 that the tide turned. The Shroud was

once more exposed for public view; and this time not for three days, but for three whole weeks. Scientists and scholars were allowed to scrutinize it repeatedly and for hours at a time, some of them even to handle it. Commander Enrie, an expert photographer, took twelve photographs under the most carefully calculated conditions and with the best equipment available. And, as if still further to dispel the doubts of the sceptics, there came from the four corners of the world 2,000,000 pilgrims to offer their homage. The photographs, which were officially guaranteed to be technically perfect, not only confirmed those of Pia, they went still further. They reversed once and for all the tide of intellectual opinion.

"Today the investigation not only continues: it has become a complete science on its own—the science of sindonology. The old objection of the historians is still voiced by a few of the sceptics, as was for a time a further one based on a mistranslation of one word in the twentieth chapter of St. John. But this is the worst they can do. After fifty-six years of opposition they have nothing new to offer, not one single alternative to the fourteenth-century painter who confessed to so astonishing a work of art. And of the fifty documents that they once quoted in their support, forty-nine have now had to be discounted, so that there are few scholars left who seriously dispute the Shroud.

"For all this, however, the Shroud has lost neither its riddle nor its challenge. It still contains a part that science can explain and a part that science cannot explain. It challenges us to give it our attention: yet it defies us to penetrate its secrets. It attracts us with its haunting, beautiful face: yet it overawes us with its expression of power and majesty. On it we see a man who has died in unspeakable suffering, yet who remains unbroken and almost unmoved: a man who is dead, and yet somehow not dead, as though in command of death itself: a man with whom we feel perfectly at home, yet whom, if he were to call us, we could not help but obey.

"Such is the man the Holy Shroud portrays—of whom Yves Delage, the unbeliever, cried out: 'And if it be not Christ, then who is it?'"

There speaks Cheshire, the son of one of Britain's greatest jurists: the man who might have got a First in Law had he not been so preoccupied with the "dogs" and climbing Merton's walls.

There also speaks the man of supreme religious conviction: the man with a bomber pilot's life-saving capacity for shrewd and objective observation: the man whose fantastic attention to minute detail led him, as a pilot, to blacken all the interior surfaces of his cockpit and dim all the luminous dials on his instrument board so that his night vision, so essential to the swift and accurate observation of targets, was in no way impaired.

Finally, too, there speaks the man who understands ordinary people.

"The man in the street nowadays," he told me, "likes *material* confirmation of great religious events."

By this time I knew Cheshire very well indeed. "You're not averse to a spot of material confirmation yourself," I pointed out. For a moment he looked taken aback. Then his eyes crinkled, his smile spread mischievously all over his face and with that ringing hoot of laughter of his he declared:

"You know, you're right. I hadn't thought of that!"

* * *

With the buses now running smoothly Cheshire himself, as ever, was content to leave the actual running of them in the hands of his delegates and to move on to something else, though, as with all his projects, he still identified himself entirely with it and his heart was entirely behind it.

Ever since he had retrieved Arthur from his doomed bed in Petersfield Hospital, Cheshire had been acutely conscious of the spiritually comfortless days that inevitably lie in store for those who are incurably·ill and await their death in an institution.

Now, as a man who had himself spent eighteen months in a sanatorium, he understood even better all those comforts of home and friends which even the best and kindest hospital is unable to offer its inmates. To someone like himself, mentally active and determined soon to escape his bonds of invalidism the emotional sterility of a sick-bed was not so difficult. But to someone condemned to death, and only to escape his hospital bed when death itself took him away, Cheshire appreciated that the situation was ghastly.

Abruptly, then, he decided to do something about it. People came to visit him and before they left he always asked:

"You don't know of a large house going cheap, do you? I want one for a new Home."

They all offered to enquire.

"That's very kind of you," he would comment, and so, confident that since there was a great need a great offer would arrive, he lay back and waited.

Soon his confidence was justified. A big home in Manchester was his for the asking. His trustees examined it and said no, it was not suitable. Gratefully but firmly Cheshire refused the gift; and then lay back to await the next offer.

Soon it arrived. A big old house in Bromley, just what he wanted. Swiftly he accepted, set about organizing a staff and management, laid down the principle that it was for the aged and incurably sick and then, with the Home set firmly on the rails to success, removed himself from the administrative scene entirely. He had no doubt that there were plenty more schemes for him to initiate without him driving his helpers mad by interfering in the running of those already well established.

And, as so often happens with this elusive, quicksilver mind of his, it was a chance event that set him off on his next project.

He had planned about four others in the meantime, all quite horrifying in their complex difficulty, and been promptly argued out of each in succession by the many friends he invariably consults and, strangely enough, whose advice he invariably accepts. Unlike most people, Cheshire does not seek advice as a sycophantic approval of what he has already thoroughly determined to do anyway.

In any event, here are the facts. He had undergone three severe chest operations and now, at last, with a tube in his left lung, was thought to be on the mend. It was May 1954, and he had been told that he might be well and out of hospital by June.

He had been allowed to get up and dress and wander round the sanatorium's magnificent grounds and now, suddenly, came the superb news that he was well enough to leave the hospital and go home for a day. All his family and friends rejoiced in the news.

He returned to the sanatorium on the Monday jubilant and triumphant. He had visited Le Court and seen all his patients and had seen, too, the superb job done on his behalf and in his long absence by his loyal trustees. The outing had done him no physical damage, so it seemed, wherefore the doctors agreed to grant him regular Saturday leaves.

It was a curious set of events that ensued the following week-end. The prime cause of these events was the phenomenal success achieved by his display in the bus and the portrait contained in the Shroud of Turin.

Crowds that had been numbered in tens now entered the bus in their hundreds. Questions that had been shy were now eager and ardent. And with the enthusiasm of the little man came the answer to Cheshire of many of his personal problems: of how to fulfil his life's purpose not only of helping those who suffered illness but also of attacking evil: of how to link his mission to relieve suffering with his mission to restore belief in God: of how to combat the threat of war.

Lourdes was a centre of pilgrimage of those who were ill: it was also a centre of a splendid religious ceremony, a shrine of the Church. Finally it was one of the places where it was believed that the Virgin Mary had, in our times, herself appeared and offered not only spiritual consolation but also a warning against godlessness and the disasters such a godlessness would bring to the world.

Abruptly Cheshire decided that he must visit Lourdes. It was against the interests of his health and certainly against the wishes of the sanatorium staff who nursed him so devotedly. Nevertheless, he felt there were larger issues than Cheshire and Cheshire's health at stake. Lourdes represented faith, healing and a positive warning of the menace of the godless. It represented all that was important in his life, nursing, the Church and the struggle to prevent war.

So, mysteriously and to the consternation of his doctors, on this first week-end leave after eighteen months' illness, Cheshire flew to Lourdes, and on the Monday returned to the hospital.

"It's a terrific spiritual experience," Cheshire related unrepentantly of his escapade on his return. The mass pilgrimage, the procession, the devout though undemanding hopes of all those physically-shattered invalids who attended—all of these made a profound impression on the sensitive Cheshire mind. As so often happens with this extraordinary man, the joy he derived from his visit was not due to personal betterment but from the astonishing comfort that Lourdes lent to the *other* pilgrims who went there.

Of his own experience he said: "I must admit much of my own sense of exaltation vanished when I found myself clad only in a damp towel and standing in icy water up to my knees for about ten minutes. I was frozen!"

So he returned from Lourdes with the tube still in his chest and his lung still unhealed. But he had learnt a salutary lesson. The value of Lourdes lies not so much in its physical healing but in its spiritual consolation. The mind as well as the body can be strengthened, and the mind is more important than the clay that embodies it. That is the constant miracle of Lourdes.

That is why, after his return, Cheshire's next visitor, even though he knew Cheshire in all his wild exuberance and extravagance extremely well, was more than surprised when, in reply to the question "anything you want?" the cheerful Group Captain replied: "Yes—an aeroplane!"

And he did want an aeroplane—also a volunteer crew and ground staff. For what? To fly regular consignments of the sick to Lourdes.

"It was a magnificent experience for me," he explains. "Why shouldn't others share in it just because it costs more than they can afford to get there?"

He has not yet been given his aeroplane, though your writer is too shaken by Cheshire's astonishing faith to doubt that he will eventually get one, but he has already organized monthly charter flights across to Lourdes. Those who want may make the pilgrimage for £18 a head, all in. And for those who can't afford £18—well, Cheshire gets them there somehow, even if he has to get them there first and worry about the money afterwards.

There, then, in four Homes that provide a new life of cheer and comfort to cripples, the chronically sick, the neurotic, the aged and the dying, and in a monthly flight of a plane full of invalids, is the work achieved, in positive, concrete terms of helping the sick, by the man who is so often said to be "round the bend." Sometimes I would like to be round there with him.

Chapter Eighteen

FAITH

INEVITABLY, from the story that has gone before, many questions arise. They are the questions that are always asked about Cheshire. Therefore it would be just as well to answer some of them here.

"Why is he always skipping from one plan to another?" people ask. "All this business of mushrooms, trips to the moon, studying physics, colonies, homes, buses, and air-lifts to Lourdes. Why doesn't he get one project and stick to it?"

It was once written of John Barrymore, regarded by many as the greatest Hamlet of them all, that "he was never late and never made excuses. To him perfection was the aim and its attainment could not be too much trouble. He loved creating a part and, once that excitement had passed, the part interested him no more. He was not the actor who wanted to recline on a long run ... The creative part of the theatre he loved. Its repetition was unbearable."

Substitute "crusader" for "actor," "project" for "part" and "social welfare" for "theatre," and there you have a perfect definition of Cheshire. I thank Lionel Barrymore for making it, even though it was intended for his brother.

It is not fecklessness that drives Cheshire to create a Home and then, when all is running smoothly, hand it over to his trustees and himself move on to other things. He has lost none of his love for the plan simply because he no longer nurses patients and himself digs holes in the ground for a tank that promptly floats. His interest in his creation is no more dead than was Barrymore's in the character of Hamlet. It is just that, having planned and perfected it, he then prefers to let others attend to the continuation of it whilst he plans and perfects something else.

Barrymore would have been far less of an actor had he only created his Hamlet and then done nothing else but repeat that rôle, even though it was superb, for the rest of his life: so would Cheshire be far less of a crusader did he remain content simply to foster for ever the one Home at Le Court. It is in the very unfaltering momentum with which he moves briskly from one idea to the next that his strength and value lies.

This is doubly so because Cheshire is terrifyingly prolific in his ideas and admits frankly that more than half of them are awful! Fortunately, he has the capacity to reject, modify or delegate any of these ideas according to the advice of his friends or the state of their advancement. And no man ever accepted and acted upon advice more sincerely than he does. It is a brilliant man who can continuously conceive new plans: it is a big man who can, upon the urgings of others, abandon them as worthless.

"Administration never was my long suit," he explains, "but I always thought I was full of bright ideas." So he has decided that whenever the ideas are good he will put them into effect: but, having done so, their administration is much better left to others. Remembering the doggedness with which he flew one hundred missions throughout the war when, a dozen times, he could have left flying duties for others much less arduous, one cannot doubt his ability to stick to routine if he thinks he should. Nor his sincerity when now he claims to achieve more by not sticking only to one routine project.

"Besides," he adds, "I can't run these places single-handed from hospital; and if I've got helpers then I mustn't interfere with what they do. Always be wanting to make them do things my way if I did. Probably make an awful mess of it anyhow."

Hence, in the last eighteen months, three buses, a course in theology, a new Home in existence, another being negotiated and his air-lift of the sick to Lourdes. In the next eighteen months doubtless there will be even more. And in the next eighteen years the whole of Britain will probably be incorporated in the Cheshire Foundation! Who cares? It might even be a good thing, anyway.

Then people look at his Homes and his ideals, at his belief in communal living and his reiteration that, to live well, one must love thy neighbour as thyself, and promptly they demand, with deep suspicion: "Is Cheshire a Communist?"

He is not only not a Communist, he is, as one would expect in a person of his faith, fanatically anti-Communist. One of his *less* sound, suddenly-conceived ideas was that he should go and live in India. Why? Because India is a breeding-ground for Communism and he, for one, he thought, should go there and attempt to combat it.

An attractive offer of regular support for his London bus, at a time when he felt very acutely the need for support, was rejected promptly and summarily because it was made by a rather Bohemian group of people whom he suspected of being Communists. Upon checking up he found his suspicions justified, but he was not prepared to run the risk of it even before he was certain of their politics.

Equally he opposes Fascism, Nazism and all the neo-isms. Early in his career as a colonist he was approached by a gentleman from just such a neo-Nazi organization. Again he needed support. Typically, he listened to all the gentleman's arguments, which suggested somewhat ingenuously that we should all try to help one another and that the colony would flourish much more quickly with this society's aid. "Certainly not," rejected Cheshire, and proceeded, untainted, to founder on his own.

People see or read that he has created four Homes, owned a private aeroplane and drove Alfa Romeos, and they ask cynically: "What's he get out of it. Pretty wealthy bloke, this Cheshire, isn't he?"

Almost all of Leonard Cheshire's wealth vanished to pay off debts of honour incurred by his colony. His last asset, Le Court, now belongs to the Foundation and, in any event, since it "collapsed to the ground" and has been rebuilt by the Carnegie Trust, it no longer exists as the original Le Court anyway.

His only possessions are his tape recorders, his few religious books, a sports coat and slacks and Sister Theophila's bed-jacket. He is not even remotely interested in wealth or chattels and if ever he earns or is given any money he at once hands it over to his trustees or spends it on some ninety-years-old lady on the principle that "thy need is greater than mine."

As for the acquisition of it, a necessary matter when one considers that Le Court alone needs about £3,500 a year over and above guaranteed income, he relies absolutely on a blind and terrifying faith that it will come.

His accountant arrives, distraught and gloomy as anyone must be who understands debits and credits in these modern times, and says: "We're in trouble. We owe £50. What are we going to do?"

"When is it due?" demands Cheshire.

"Next Friday," and it is already Tuesday.

"Then worry me about it on Friday," instructs the good Group Captain. And always, by every Friday when it has been needed so far, the money (usually from a stranger) has arrived. It has happened so often now that even the accountant is beginning to assume that it always will. It happens, apparently, purely because of Cheshire's sublime conviction that it must.

Faith, it is said, can move mountains. Cheshire's would move the National Debt!

Other people again, perplexed that any mortal can earn so many decorations and still survive to live in the unexalted air which ordinary citizens breathe, ask: "Was he ever afraid? I don't suppose he could have been."

Cheshire himself has answered that question in various ways. Of his lack of fear over Munich he pointed out that he had been so preoccupied with ordering bombs down that he *forgot* that he was in danger, and remarked that "that made it difficult to assess courage, didn't it?"

At Antheor, although he attacked seven times running in the face of vicious and concentrated fire, a sustained effort that we, the undecorated masses, would regard as courageous and determined in the extreme, he declares bluntly that he lost his nerve.

But the whole matter of courage and the lack of it he summed up best when called, in 1953, to comment upon the court martial of a British serviceman for cowardice in Korea. This is what he said:

"What makes a man a coward—or a hero? Before the war I used to puzzle about that a lot. I used to ask myself how, if the big test came, I would stand up to it. *I still wonder—and I still don't know.* Because the fact that you've survived once successfully doesn't mean you'll do so again.

"The first time I found myself under fire in the air came in 1940. We were on a bombing mission behind the lines over Dunkirk. I was in a Whitley bomber—a member of another man's crew. I was so concerned not to let anyone else know that I was frightened that I had no time to bother about anything else. Being part of a crew helped. Outwardly at least, my companions didn't seem to be worried, and I couldn't help catching some of their spirit.

"The main thing I remember about that trip was the tiredness I felt afterwards. Of course we didn't have much opposition to contend with at that time. You might say I was 'blooded' gently.

"*But, you know, fear in itself doesn't greatly matter. It's an animal reaction that we all experience at some time or other.* What matters is that we should overcome that fear. It's an insidious business. It grows with every mission, every new adventure into danger. And it's the constant effort to beat it that keeps every nerve strained. There comes a time when every one of us has had enough.

"When I finally came off operational flying I was somewhat indignant with the doctors. I thought I was good for a long time yet. So did the other men in the squadron. But after we had been forcibly removed from the flying list we began to relax. The measure of that relaxation told us, for the first time, just how near to breaking point we had been.

"First you've got to think of this thing in relation to other people. Fear and courage are alike infectious. If a man is a member of a unit, and suddenly shows cowardice, obviously the authorities have got to do something—and quickly—before he affects his comrades. Similarly if he shows bravery, this, too, should be recognized appropriately."

There is his public testimony on fear. Privately he never hesitates to express his disappointment that the system of recognizing courage officially so often means only that a figure-head is chosen on behalf of a group and that the decoration then goes to him. "My V.C.," he states emphatically, "was for 617 Squadron." And there can be no doubt, when he says it, that that is exactly what he means.

*   *   *

So there is your most decorated hero of the war today. An ordinary man in appearances with an extraordinarily fertile brain. An intensely religious man with a great power to attract towards good things even those who are intensely irreligious. A devout man who retains an earthy sense of humour and a delightful—even, occasionally, a mad—sense of fun. A total invalid for two years who, in that two years, has done more work than any dozen of us less fortunate healthy people put together.

He has been described as a saint. It is a word I do not like. It implies something apart, someone not quite like ordinary people, and yet that is Cheshire's greatest charm, that, being wholly extraordinary, he has this capacity to remain completely in touch with the common man. It implies an austere severity, yet Cheshire is gloriously and incorrigibly frivolous. It implies, worst of all, this being a saint, that one is dead— and Cheshire is vitally, abundantly and prodigiously alive.

As a flyer he was conspicuously brave and successful and a born leader. The war proved to others, but, more important, to him as well, that he could do something supremely well. Then came Nagasaki and the end of the conflict.

It is all his war-time qualities of adaptability, attention to detail, the willingness coldly to take risks in the interests of a cause, the ability to persuade others to his way of reasoning, to lead others along his way of action; it is all these qualities, fortified with a strong religious faith and humanized always by his irrepressible humour, that he brings now to his peace-time crusade of "loving God above everything and thy neighbour as thyself."

The only question that remains to be asked about him, of course, is: "where does he go from here?"

The cynics declare that, since he has embraced and then abandoned so many other causes, he will inevitably abandon the Roman Catholic Church as well.

The answer to that statement lies in the future and in the heart of Leonard Cheshire. Yet this much is certain. He is a man upon whom has fallen an aura of complete tranquillity and serenity. He is sublimely happy in his faith.

He is so happy in it that he has none of the doubter's need to convince himself by convincing others. He makes no attempt to "sell" his religion. It is only fair to comment that all the arguments adduced in this book in favour of Roman Catholicism were obtained from him under cross-examination and were given by him not as aggressive arguments against other religions but only as an explanation of his own conversion.

No ear could have been less biased in favour of Catholicism than mine. When I met Cheshire I was a complete heathen. I remain one today. This worried him not at all (indeed he seemed to enjoy it) and he made no attempt at any stage to convince me of the disastrous error of my ways.

Proof of this tolerance lies in the fact that all his Homes, Le Court, St. Teresa's, Holy Cross and St. Cecilia's, are nonsectarian. The qualification for those who have entered these Homes, and for those who wait, is not a religious one; it is merely that they be sick and in need of help. Once, even, it was merely that they knocked on the door and asked to be taken in.

In the light of such personal joy in his own faith, and of such detached calm about the faith of others, it does not seem probable that he will please the cynics by eventually forsaking the Church of Rome. But whatever his future course he will steer it with courage.

On one count at least, however, anyone with a critical mind *can* join issue with Cheshire. That is his affirmation of authority as an argument in favour of his becoming a Catholic. Look at Cheshire's life and his attitude towards authority throughout.

At school..."I was rather a trial—bit unorthodox. Can't remember how, but I know I was." In Germany in 1935 ... he refused to salute a military parade. In Oxford from 1936–39 ... a car that was against college regulations, constant visits to London to the "dogs" and equally constant returns to college over the wall. During the war ... hated cockpit drill: frequently bombed below the level ordered because he couldn't stand heights: planned to drop food over a prisoner-of-war compound without any official sanction: stood up to men, often his seniors in rank and experience, and never hesitated to back his judgment even when it might have been diplomatic to toe the line.

Even today, after four savage operations, as he recuperates from tuberculosis, he plans to outwit and circumvent the medical edicts laid down for his future.

"You must spend quite some time just staying at home," he has been told. So what does he intend doing? Staying in his home, by all means: but that home will be a station-wagon equipped with bed, desk, filing-cabinet, tape-recorder and public address system which will enable him to move round and work freely all over the country.

"All they said was that *I* mustn't move," he explains. "They didn't say anything about my home!" Here again the lawyer's training, and the application of the same principle exactly as allowed him, with easy conscience, to fly to Lourdes.

All of this I pointed out to him. He smiled delightedly throughout. So then, bluntly, I asked the question everyone wants to ask: "Since you've always defied or altered authority all your life, when it clashed with your own convictions, what is going to happen if ever your convictions clash with the authority of the Roman Catholic Church? Actually I don't think you have much respect for authority, as such, at all!"

The keen eyes gleamed and crinkled, and the pursed mouth spread into a wide, schoolboy's grin.

"Well I don't know about that one," he answered easily. "But, fortunately, I'm sure it'll never happen."

Looking at him, as he smiles like this, one remembers that not only his grin is boyish. He has the child's directness of approach to a subject, the child's uncomplicated acceptance of facts that work. And, for him, religion works.

All his post-war projects are motivated by this basic urge to ease the complexities and centralization of modern life—to return to the more fundamental and simpler principles of living together. Both his faith and his interpretation of the teachings of Christ seem wholly to be based on the maxim "except ye be as a child ye shall not enter the kingdom of heaven." And this philosophy, like aerodynamics or Law, is one, Cheshire feels confidently, that he has studied, mastered and can now put into practical effect.

He may be wrong. His boundless enthusiasm and his ambitious imagination may tempt him to a task that wrecks itself on the rock of spiritual pride. His generous desire to please everyone and to be agreeable to all may cause him suddenly to please none and to find the whole world in disagreement with him. But his past record does not seem to indicate that. And, even if it were to happen, he has faced disaster so often in the air, and with his V.I.P. scheme, and overcome unpopularity so often with the powers who administered in Bomber Command, or those who said that he was mad, that surely he would survive it.

Against the remote possibility of some future setback lie the facts that, in a world of uncertainty and fear, Cheshire is confident and unafraid: in an age where so many people today grope hopefully for some spiritual consolation, Cheshire has found it: at a time when all the virtues men revealed during the war seem to have vanished into oblivion, Cheshire is exploiting his own more determinedly than ever: that in answer to all those who demand: "What's the use? What can

I do?'', Cheshire has found something to do and gone out and done it. And there are almost a hundred people, once helpless and hopeless, now living happy lives in his four Homes to prove it.

Of one man in one lifetime nobody can ask more than that. If they should do, there are his five citations for valour to satisfy even them.

ACKNOWLEDGMENTS

IN SPITE of the trying circumstances of his illness, Leonard Cheshire granted me endless bedside interviews, in the course of which he told me his story in words so well chosen that often all I had to do was take them down and insert them intact into my manuscript. For that, for his patience, kindness and friendship, and for his revision of this completed work, I am grateful.

Also I must acknowledge my indebtedness to Wilfrid Walter who did so much of the preliminary research work behind the story: to *Picture Post* for making available copies of their photographs: to Mrs. Cheshire, Group Captain Cheshire's mother, for having made available family snapshots: to Professor G. C. Cheshire for his careful correction of some early errors: to Air Ministry Information for their goodwill in answering questions they must have been asked a thousand times: and to the national Press—particularly the *Daily Sketch*, the *Sunday Graphic*, the *News Chronicle*, the *Daily Herald*, *The Times* and the *Sunday Pictorial*—for permission to quote from or use information supplied in articles in their pages. Special thanks are due to Messrs. Hutchinson for permission to quote several extracts and pieces of dialogue from the book *Bomber Pilot* by Group Captain Cheshire.

For background material I had recourse to a number of books—*The Dam Busters* by Paul Brickhill: *For Valour* by Kenneth Hare Scott: *The History of the R.A.F.* 1939–45, Vols. 1 and 2: *V.2.* by Major-General Walter Dornberger:

Sir Winston Churchill's *Second World War*, Vols. V and VI: *Enemy Coast Ahead* by Guy Gibson, V.C.: *The Face of a King* by Veronica: Leonard Cheshire's booklet *The Holy Face*.

It is worth noting that a more exhaustive work on Group Captain Cheshire's career and present crusade is now in preparation. Its author is Andrew Boyle, a friend of Leonard Cheshire and a fellow Roman Catholic.